Fine Interiors

OF NAPLES, FLORIDA

LAURI GARBO

Copyright © 2003 by Twin Lights Publishers, Inc.
and Yourtown Books

All rights reserved. No part of this book may be reproduced in any form without written permission of the copyright owners. All images in this book have been reproduced with the knowledge and prior consent of the artists concerned and no responsibility is accepted by producer, publisher, or printer for any infringement of copyright or otherwise, arising from the contents of this publication. Every effort has been made to ensure that credits accurately comply with information supplied.

First published in the United States of America by:

Twin Lights Publishers, Inc.
10 Hale Street
Rockport, Massachusetts 01966
Telephone: (978) 546-7398
http://www.twinlightspub.com

and

Yourtown Books
Naples, Florida
Telephone: (239) 825-1277

ISBN 1-885435-41-X

10 9 8 7 6 5 4 3 2 1

Book design by
SYP Design & Production, Inc.
http://www.sypdesign.com

Printed in China

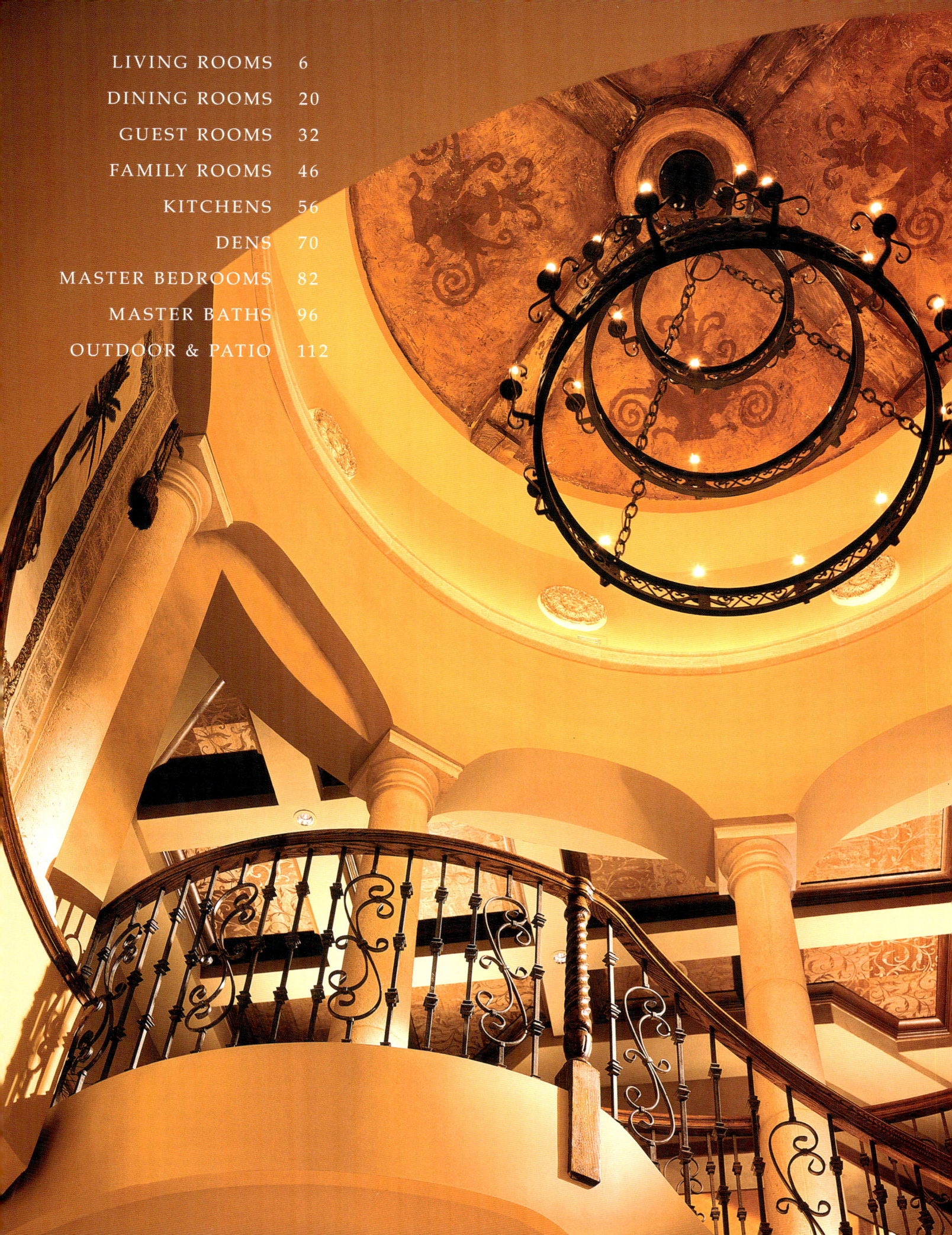

LIVING ROOMS 6
DINING ROOMS 20
GUEST ROOMS 32
FAMILY ROOMS 46
KITCHENS 56
DENS 70
MASTER BEDROOMS 82
MASTER BATHS 96
OUTDOOR & PATIO 112

INTRODUCTION

The Naples real estate market boomed in the 1980s, and the echoes of prosperity are still being heard today. Original, low profile ranch homes succumbed to lavish mansions that emerged not only in the waterfront estates of Port Royal, but throughout Collier County's golf course communities and surrounding areas as well.

Retired CEOs, affluent baby boomers, and seasonal residents have commissioned grand estates that possess the best of everything—state-of-the-art home theaters, commercial-style kitchens, private fitness facilities, expansive master suites, and lavish outdoor living areas that take advantage of the balmy subtropical climate. Individual style has replaced the stiff, predictable model-home look, and unlimited budgets and sky's-the-limit imaginations have taken home interiors to a new, personalized level.

Living rooms have developed a character all their own. Classical details have returned in the forms of mantels, molding and trim, stately columns, custom paneling and splendid ceiling treatments. Imparting style and warmth, architectural detailing adds visual interest and richness to the interior. From lavish expressions of opulence to refined statements of casual elegance, living rooms present the initial welcome.

As a static showpiece or a dynamic domain, the dining room continues to command attention. The setting for sumptuous holiday dinners, festive gatherings, and spontaneous celebrations also receives meticulous attention from ceiling medallions to dramatic, faux finish details.

Because having a home in Naples is like extending a year-round invitation to friends and relatives, a necessary amenity is a private guest suite. Guest suites have become more sophisticated, and the design elements have followed suit with distinctive furnishings, carefully selected fabrics, and colors that subtly blend to communicate a heart-felt welcome. Luxurious furnishings once reserved for the master of the home, are being offered graciously to extended family and friends.

As the nucleus of the home, kitchens meld communication, entertainment, and creative endeavors in one stylish control center where meal preparation used to be paramount. Today's fast-paced lives demand the multipurpose kitchen that centers on a homeowner's need to be quick and efficient. The mere size of kitchen space testifies to its multifaceted uses. Separate yet unified work spaces allow for varied activities and maximum versatility. Style has not been forgotten here. Granite countertops, fine wood cabinetry in a variety of glazed and antiqued finishes, and elaborate range hoods define the unique personality of the space.

Yesterday's study has become today's multifunctional home office. An abundance of technological equipment now mingles within the soothing space where novels are read and world journeys are planned. Leather, wood, and heavily textured fabrics are the initial ingredients that form a comfortable library or study. Recent trends reflect the cultural diversity and global adventures of residents who now call Naples home.

Seeking solitude and luxury, the dimensions and amenities of the master suite have become paramount to homeowners. In the most elaborate homes, master suites sprawl to include an adjacent fitness cove, wet bar, entertainment center, cozy sitting area, and personal spa.

From sophisticated powder baths to elaborate master spas, the bathroom has become a luxurious space where individuals can pamper themselves. Design inspirations are limitless from the classic to the contemporary. Aged stone surfaces, majestic columns, custom cabinetry, and stylish fixtures combine to create unique environments specifically suited to the homeowners' needs.

The desire to blend interior and exterior living spaces has inspired an outdoor living trend that incorporates summer kitchens, sprawling loggias, and poolside gazebos ideal for intimate dining beneath the stars.

Each room in this unique collection of fine interiors was created with the professional guidance of an interior designer and illustrates an unwavering attention to detail and style.

LIVING ROOMS

Left

HUNT CONSTRUCTION CO., INC.
VINCE-MULLER
INTERIOR DESIGN

Extensive architectural detail creates a resounding statement in this magnificent living room. The fireplace detail combines natural shellstone and drywall recesses to provide dramatic depth. The unique accessories were collected from the designer's extensive world travel. Hand-embroidered silk draperies add rich color as they frame the French doors that lead to the pool and reflecting pond beyond.

Below

ROBB & STUCKY
BARBARA ELLIS, ASID, FLORIDA
LICENSED INTERIOR DESIGNER

Indulgent chenille and silk upholstery evoke comfort and warmth in this formal living room. A guilded pedestal coffee table and romantic chaise add to the luxurious feel created by the swagged silk window coverings. A painting by a Russian artist enhances the mood.

Opposite

ROBB & STUCKY
BETTI WALCOTT, ASID, FLORIDA
LICENSED INTERIOR DESIGNER

Masculine design choices and colors project a formal and bold statement. Dramatic window coverings spotlight the pool outside and provide a symmetrical backdrop for the rest of the room. Black and gold tones run throughout the silk plaid table cover, custom area rug with a black border, a pair of wood-framed chenille sofas, handsome upholstered chairs, and antique pine coffee table.

Photo credit: Barry J. Grossman

LIVING ROOMS

Right

HOLLAND SALLEY INTERIOR DESIGN
LISA FICARRA SHEPHERD, ALLIED MEMBER, ASID

The overall design concept combines the unique influence of French and Italian details. The living room boasts an elegant, yet unintimidating environment, a place in which to relax in front of the beautiful stone fireplace while gazing at the bay through the magnificent floor to ceiling windows framed with formal swagged draperies. Subtle shades of celadon, parsnip, champagne and melon flow throughout the home, subtle in some areas and stronger in others.

Photo credit: Jennifer Deane

Below

ACCESSORIES ETC., INC.

Rich-hued blue walls and custom wood built-ins and fireplace mantel accented with crisp, white upholstered furnishings create a dramatic flair in this Southwest Florida living room. The conversational-minded seating area is anchored with a unique oriental carpet.

Photo credit: Jim Freeman

Opposite

COLLINS & DUPONT INTERIORS, INC.
KIM COLLINS, ASID

A grand two-story living room offers a dramatic focal point where design symmetry and architectural detail merge. Semicircular balconies look down upon the overstuffed chenille sofas, dark wood and glass cocktail table, and arm chair. A gas fireplace with a decorative iron screen and stone mantel anchor the room.

Photo credit: Laurence Taylor

10   FINE INTERIORS OF NAPLES, FLORIDA

Left

ACCESSORIES ETC., INC.

This grand salon features 26-foot ceilings and natural marble columns and details. The color palette is reminiscent of the Tuscan hillside—warm umber and terra cotta accented by sea tones of cerulean. The oversized, chenille-covered sofa creates a gracious setting that invites guests to linger. An exquisite Oriental rug adds warmth and softness to the marble floors. (*Builder, Frey & Sons Homes*)

Photo credit: Jim Freemam

Below

DON EWY CONSTRUCTION, INC.

This grand entry doubles as a dining room. The teak entry door and teak framed windows draw attention to the cypress, beamed ceiling structure. Antique Asian artifacts flank the entry near a pair of keystone columns.

Photo credit: Carl Thome

Opposite

FREESTYLE INTERIORS
FAITH FIX, ASID

This single-family estate home features a contemporary interpretation of Mediterranean architecture. Similar to villas in Italy, the living room incorporates a coffered ceiling and a majestic curved stone wall, which gracefully enhances the high arched windows overlooking the lagoon pool. This grandiose entry with 22-foot high shell stone columns, and a custom inlay stone detail in the foyer, invites guests into a luxurious living room with gold, hand-painted silk and rich wine-colored tapestry fabrics, and a one-of-a-kind iron and glass oversized lighting fixture, thus setting the tone for formal entertaining.

LIVING ROOMS   13

Right

THE THOMAS RILEY
ARTISANS' GUILD

A hand-crafted masterpiece, this bar is created from plain sliced mahogany, with cross-banded Sapelle mahogany around the panels, and crotch-cut, book-matched, mahogany panels. The hand-carved details and leaded glass insets reflect exquisite craftsmanship and tradition.

The view from the custom-built mahogany bar area, provides a unique perspective of this stately great room that highlights a grand piano and richly appointed furnishings.

Below

THE THOMAS RILEY
ARTISANS' GUILD

A black grand piano is balanced with accents of imperial blue and red. Artisans designed the piano bar, installed the crown and base moldings that delineate the space, and adorned the ceiling and walls with decorative stippling in metallic gold and silver. Two lustrous chandeliers add greater formality to the room.

Opposite

DON EWY CONSTRUCTION, INC.

A rustic Mediterranean design creates an inviting foyer and living area. The stairway is comprised of sturdy turned spindles in a dark old Tuscan finish, and the risers are ivory cream honed and unfilled natural stone with distressed edges. An Italian medallion at front entry and pecky cypress ceiling imbue an authentic countryside aura. Earth tones in the upholstery and an aged finish on the walls further enhance the setting.

Photo credit: Dyehouse Comeriato

14   FINE INTERIORS OF NAPLES, FLORIDA

Left

HOLLAND SALLEY
INTERIOR DESIGN
LINDA BURKE, ASID, NCIDQ

The Neoclassical architectural details accented by abstract artwork and streamlined furniture mesh contemporary and traditional elements to form a richly styled, comfortable interior. The background color palette comprised of soft, cool tints of blue, green and yellow accents the dark wood and metal furniture and textural upholstery. The living room's sense of luxury is further enhanced through the use of glass shelves in the wet bar, crystal stemware, and colorful art resting within metallic silver insets.

Photo credit: Nick Shirghio

Below

COLLINS & DUPONT
INTERIORS, INC.
SHERRON P. DUPONT, ASID

A neutral palette of creams and soft golden tones creates a sophisticated living room setting. Conversation is encouraged with an abundance of seating options on two upholstered sofas with silk pillows and two chairs. As a contrast to the luxurious light fabrics, dark wood tables and an iron-gated wine cellar offer visual interest.

Photo credit: Laurence Taylor

Opposite

HOLLAND SALLEY INTERIOR DESIGN
JOHN BELLOWS, ASID

This room represents a Bermuda-style home that is inviting and comfortable. The design concept for the sitting room of this guest suite began with the dark navy and white print for the pair of lounge chairs. These chairs have a clear glass, hand-blown table between them which can be used for drinks, accessories, or personal photos. In order to balance the navy, the bypass shutters, crown moldings, baseboards and fireplace mantel were painted white, and the wool carpet was done in off-white. The Chippendale framed mirror was changed from gold leaf to Arctic white. Accents of cinnabar were used to give the room a touch of color on the mantle above the brass-hammered fireplace screen.

Photo credit: Carlos Domenech

LIVING ROOMS

ROZ TRAVIS INTERIORS
ROZ TRAVIS

In this chic uptown residence a distinctive trompe l' oiel portrays a view from a private cabana complete with awning and draperies. The scene supports the illusion of life in paradise.

LINDY THOMAS INTERIORS
LINDY THOMAS, ASID

Softly enhancing the charm of a cottage in Olde Naples, the periwinkle and cream colors play off the furnishings, thus, making the room light and airy. A painting by Ann Vacarro adds an abstract quality to the room.

Photo credit: Oscar Thompson

LIVING ROOMS   19

DINING ROOMS

Left

HUNT CONSTRUCTION CO., INC.

A rod iron chandelier and inlaid wood buffet are reflected in the antique mirror with rosette insets surrounded by precast stone. Leather host and hostess chairs are grouped with terra cotta and golf floral chenille guest chairs in this luxurious setting.

Below

DESIGN GROUP WEST
GLENN MIDNET, ASID, IDS

This room captures the Tuscan feel with its architectural interest created by the keystone castle block. The hand-carved dining chairs have a sophisticated look in a Stroheim and Roman taupe and black silk. The antiqued, distressed molding adds the finishing touch.

Opposite

VALENTINE & STONE INTERIORS
MICHAEL VALENTINE, ASID
AND ROBERTA VALENTINE

Extensive architectural details include a hatbox tray ceiling inset with an architectural medallion, wallpaper border, and accent paint. Ogee arches are repeated over the serving buffet, around the window and at the room's entry. Above the serving buffet, faux-look wallpaper is framed with painted molding, and exhibits a contemporary painting that contrasts the formality of the room. The serving buffet consists of two pedestals and a faux-leather top. Silver leaf finish on the dining room chairs mirrors the graceful curves of the arches.

DINING ROOMS 23

Right

LUNDIN INTERIORS, INC.
RONALD E. LUNDIN, ALLIED
ASID, ASSOC. IIDA, ASSOC. IDS

A most elegant Mediterranean tropical dining room is accented with rich, tropical hues and eclectic furnishings. A gallery painting is complemented with heavy tapestry fabrics and intricately designed window treatments. Custom iron work, which tops the window treatments, architecturally enhances the setting. This custom blend of furnishings and accessories creates Florida living at its finest.

Photo credit: Sargent

Below

PLATINUM COAST
ARTISANS & CRAFTSMEN

Dark wood furnishings, gold metallic finishes, and richly upholstered chairs come alive amidst this cranberry, custom colorwash finish. An octagon-shaped ceiling design has been treated with various faux and molding applications to complement the ornate crystal chandelier.

Opposite

ROBB & STUCKY
JOSEPHINE ALAIMO, ASID, IDS,
FLORIDA LICENSED INTERIOR
DESIGNER

Country French and Neoclassic merge in this formal dining room. Golden hues with punches of red create a regal statement. A cherub motif, requested by the owner, creates a playful scene. An antique Oriental rug under foot, a Crawford ceiling, cove moldings, and faux finishes complete the design.

Right

**FREESTYLE INTERIORS
RAGAN HARRIS**

A true sense of grandeur and elegance, enhanced by the architectural interest of applied moldings with foiled wallpaper insets, creates a dining experience on European style furniture under ambient lighting. Ondulato stone, inlaid with a metallic green slate, connects, and yet separates, the living and dining room space from the gallery foyer.

Below

**COLLINS & DUPONT
INTERIORS, INC.
SHERRON P. DUPONT, ASID**

Rich woods dominate this dining area. The ceiling treatment incorporates indirect lighting with a commanding alabaster and metal fixture. Repeating design elements from the main living areas, the designer created a niche for a beautiful wood server. Burled wood insets and distinctive metal pulls elevate the server beyond merely functional. A display cabinet for china and stemware marks the transition into the kitchen and family room beyond.

Photo credit: Laurence Taylor

Opposite

**LINDY THOMAS INTERIORS
LINDY THOMAS, ASID**

An inspiring location is put to its best use in this superb breakfast nook overlooking Venetian Bay. Motorized, natural fiber shades protect the silk draperies from the sun and inclement weather. The handmade rug is topped with a glass table and contemporary wicker seating with leather seat covers.

Photo credit: Oscar Thompson

Right

**HOLLAND SALLEY
INTERIOR DESIGN
LESLIE CHRISTIAN, ASID, NCIDQ**

Contemporary design makes a break-through on the beach in this penthouse in Naples. The breakfast room has been enlarged to use as a dining room. This allows the owner to position his baby grand piano in what was formerly the dining room. The oversized artwork helps to convey the room's importance. Walls have been penetrated to add openness and to expose existing structure as design.

Photo credit: Ed Chappell

Below

**LINDY THOMAS INTERIORS
LINDY THOMAS, ASID**

The stylish dining ensemble creates visual elegance in a simple and well-balanced design. The Florida-style shutters serve as a minimal window treatment and enhance the subtle contemporary feel to the room. An innovative ceiling feature is used to properly position the chandelier directly over the table.

Photo credit: Oscar Thompson

Opposite

**VINCE MULLER
INTERIOR DESIGN
DENISE WARD, ASID**

Carved wood table bases and chairs set the mood for this elegant dining room. The intricately carved mirror highlights the buffet and reflects the design details in the wrought iron chandelier.

Photo credit: Joseph Lapeyra Photography

FINE INTERIORS OF NAPLES, FLORIDA

Right

HOLLAND SALLEY
INTERIOR DESIGN
DINA LODEN, ALLIED
MEMBER, ASID

Mediterranean architecture of the Tuscan villa was the inspiration for this dining room. The Venetian plaster, faux finished walls are the focal point, and the botanical prints on the fabric of the chairs reflect the jewel tones used throughout the home. This warm, elegant dining room sets the mood for a delightful meal with friends.

Photo credit: Tim Stamm

Below

THE THOMAS RILEY
ARTISANS' GUILD
CHRISTIE METZ & THOMAS RILEY

One of a pair of handcrafted, dining room corner cabinets exhibits the attention to detail and artistry of this firm. The cabinet doors are created from crotch-cut mahogany. Floral marquetry and a beveled marble top and rim create a built-in look.

Opposite

ACCESSORIES ETC., INC.

The color palette that is used throughout the home was taken from strong yet soothing colors found in nature, specifically, the sunrise and sunset--sunny yellows, golds, melons, and regal-toned aubergine. The traditional mahogany dining room table and sideboard are paired with elegant teak and caned chairs. A hand-painted mural mimics the tropical ambience of the outdoors. (*Builder, Frey & Sons Homes*)

Photo credit: Jim Freeman

GUEST ROOMS

Left

LUNDIN INTERIORS
RONALD E. LUNDIN, ALLIED ASID, ASSOC, IIDA, ASSOC. IDS

This seaside retreat was created with grandchildren in mind. A pair of custom-built bunk beds free up floor space for lounging and play. The hand-painted mural depicts breezy beach scenes and inspiring wildlife. Soft denim upholstery and pale yellow bedding combine to create a cozy home-away-from-home.

Below

LINDY THOMAS INTERIORS
LINDY THOMAS, ASID

The guest suite reflects an updated, sophisticated British Colonial style. An attractive mix of periwinkle and white with a touch of yellow creates a uniquely feminine space. The hand-painted custom furniture is finely crafted and lends harmony to the room. The final touch, a crystal lamp with a prissy silk shade, further characterizes the statement.

Photo credit: Greg Wilson

Opposite

ROBB & STUCKY
BETTI WALCOTT, ASID, IDS, FLORIDA LICENSED INTERIOR DESIGNER

Children and grandchildren will delight in this cheerful sunny suite. Whimsical accents, including a lifeguard floor lamp, oversized beach ball, and yellow awning, create a fun-filled beach escape. The faux sky ceiling tops off this room with fair Southwest Florida skies.

GUEST ROOMS 35

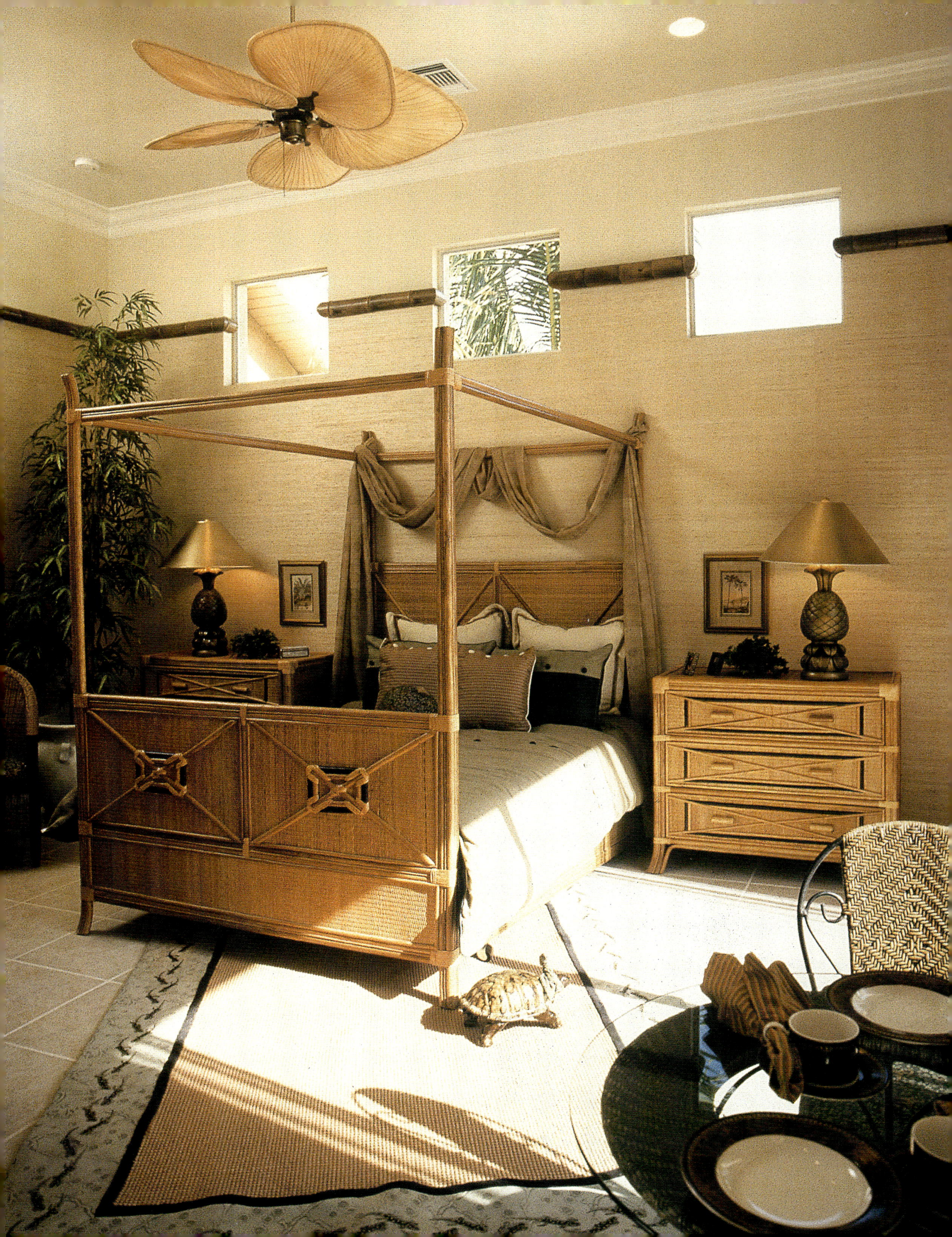

Left

DESIGN GROUP WEST
GLENN MIDNET, ASID, IDS

This room's focal point is the grand king tester bed with its custom fabricated canopy and luxurious full drapes with satin trimmed embellishments. Custom bed linens, with exquisite hand-sewn details, complete the ensemble. The bed is flanked by an antique reproduction bombe chest and a hand-selected, silver gilt framed oval mirror. The romantic flavor is further enhanced with warm incandescent lighting from the decorative lamps and lighting fixtures. The entire room, with its monochromatic finishes and fabrics lend an air of sophistication.

Below

ROBB & STUCKY
KELLI SMITH, ASID, FLORIDA LICENSED INTERIOR DESIGNER

Sumptuous fabrics, soothing colors, and Olde World styling create a luxurious haven for the consummate world traveler. The four-poster, Venetian hand-painted bed, a Robb & Stucky exclusive, and chenille upholstered, wood-exposed chairs beckon guests to linger. Custom-designed silk bedding, and silk dupione window coverings are decadent details that create a guest room which is truly inspiring.

Opposite

THERESA CAROLLO INTERIORS
THERESA A. CAROLLO,
ALLIED MEMBER, ASID

This West Indies getaway theme is complete with grass cloth, bamboo chair rail moldings, and a palm frond fan. The four-poster cane and bamboo bed, with a bedding ensemble of elephants and solid colors of linen, green, beige and russet, adds to the look of an exotic getaway. The sisal area rug, bordered in tapestry of chameleons, is home for "Mr. Turtle" in this fun suite.

Photo credit: Ron Blakeley

GUEST ROOMS   37

Right

ROMANZA INTERIOR DESIGN
JENNIFER STEVENS

Sporting the luxuries of a fine European hotel, the guest suite bath provides a spacious area and trans-Atlantic amenities. Clean, functional lines combine with the curves of an old-fashioned baked enamel, soaking tub. A combination of soft faux finishes and checkered wall tile balance the space.

Photo credit: Laurence Taylor

Below

ROMANZA INTERIOR DESIGN
JENNIFER STEVENS

Clean, crisp lines and bold white trim promote a cool and casual atmosphere in this guest suite. Mirroring the natural scene beyond the verandah, this room promotes the lively, tropical spirit of Naples. Whimsical cockatoos and parrots perch on and near the bed reminding occupants of the tropical nature that surrounds them.

Photo credit: Laurence Taylor

Opposite

THERESA CAROLLO INTERIORS
THERESA A. CAROLLO,
ALLIED, ASID

The twin bedroom evokes a fun getaway feel with cute monkeys and palm trees in a light British West Indies look. The tented canopies add whimsy to the "well traveled" theme. To keep the Indies look "light," soft colors of buttercup yellow, yellow-greens, and lilacs are utilized. The coffered ceiling is covered with woven grass cloth, and the palm frond fan tops off the overall theme.

Photo credit: Ron Blakeley

38   FINE INTERIORS OF NAPLES, FLORIDA

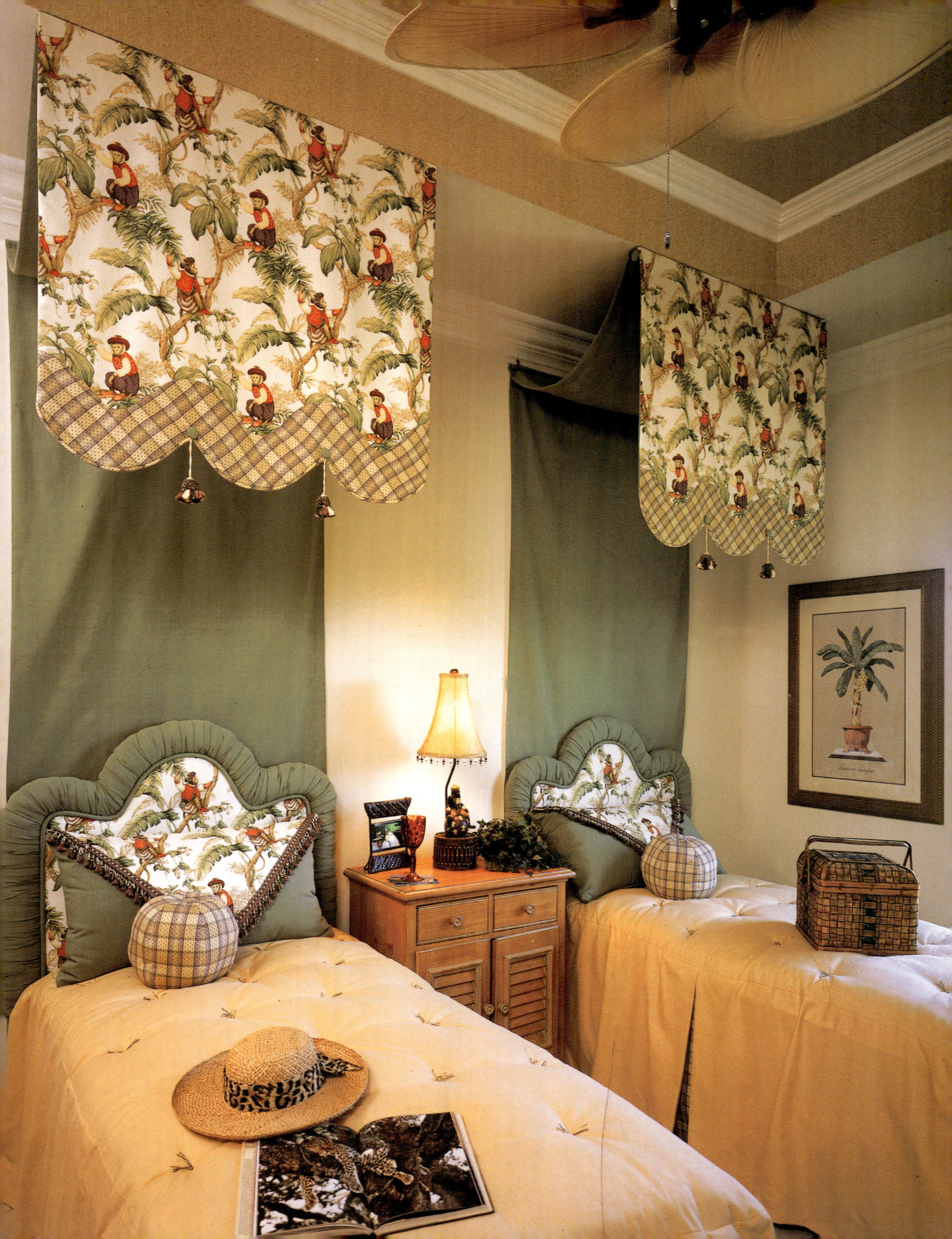

Right

FREESTYLE INTERIORS
RAGAN HARRIS

Beautiful, soft silk window treatments border the bay windows which are enhanced by the porthole above, allowing an abundance of light. Soft, muted tones create calming sensations in this classic bedroom design.

Below

DESIGN GROUP WEST
GLENN MIDNET, ASID, IDS

The understated flavor of this room was designed with the idea of a casual and serene guest suite retreat. The walls are painted in an earthy tobacco color which provides a contrast to the pale fresco-washed finish of the furniture. The over-scaled furnishings feature hand-carved details and pewter finished hardware. The bed coverings are neat and tailored with a minimum of ornament, thus showcasing a variety of textures, such as chenille, silk, and linen. The overall ambiance of the guest suite lends itself to a calm, yet sophisticated, retreat.

Opposite

HOLLAND SALLEY
INTERIOR DESIGN
JULIE A. BREZINA,
ALLIED MEMBER, ASID

Tropical with an Indonesian influence, this design concept is comparable to the British West Indies look, but unusual antique and colorful accessories give it an interesting twist. Raffia covered cornice boards, a large botanical print in a shadow box, and a hand-painted antique armoire promote the island theme while the lavish use of fabric and pillows convey a feeling of luxury.

Photo credit: Nick Shirghio

FINE INTERIORS OF NAPLES, FLORIDA

GUEST ROOMS 41

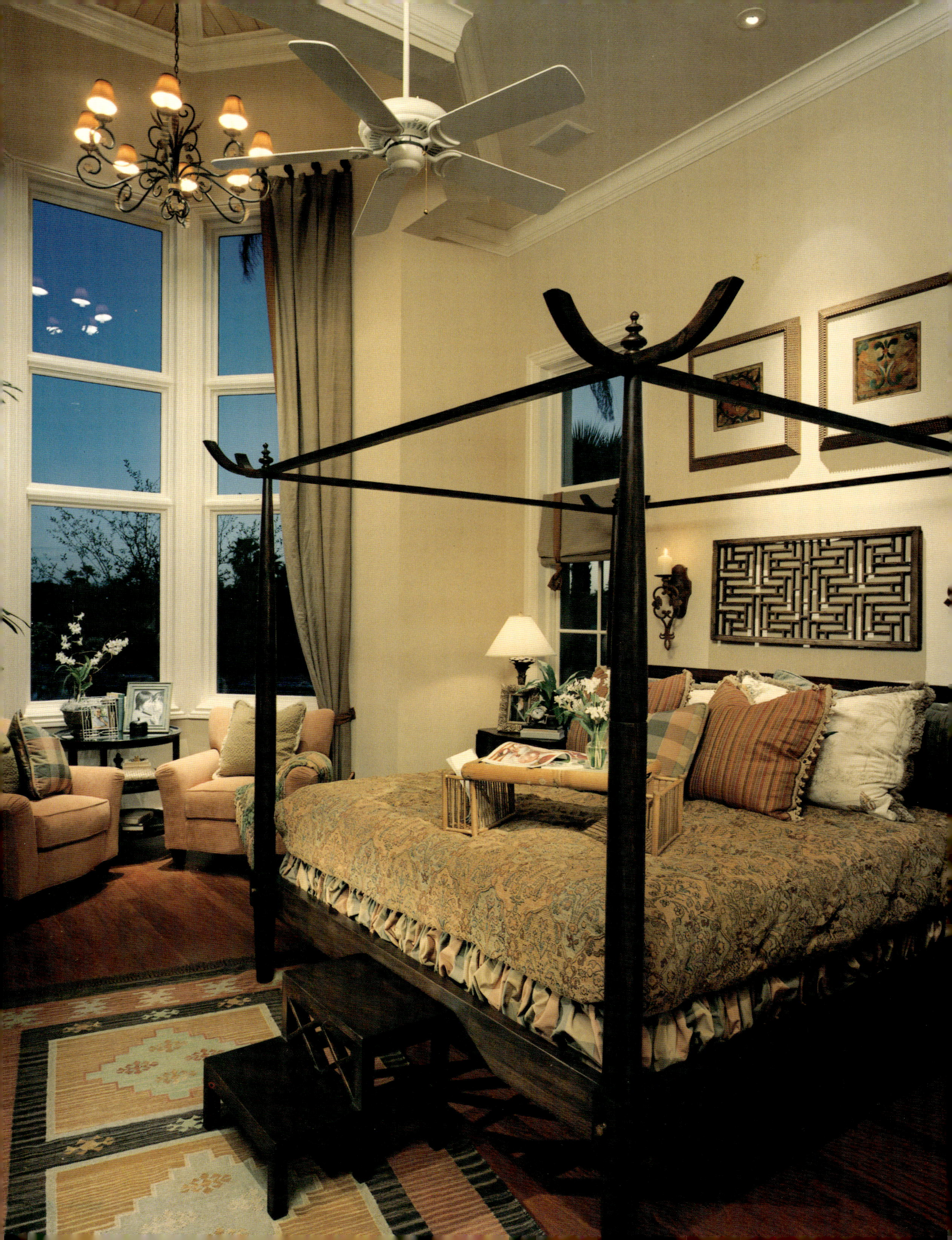

Left

**VALENTINE & STONE INTERIORS
MICHAEL VALENTINE, ASID
AND ROBERTA VALENTINE**

An Oriental, contemporary theme sets the tone for this bedroom design. Neutral colors with red and black accents provide the backdrop for dark wood furnishings. Dark lampshades on Asian-styled lamps add drama and interest. Above the bed, suede finished wallpaper, vertical mirrors, and accent painted moldings give the illusion of space and height.

Below

**HOLLAND SALLEY
INTERIOR DESIGN
JULIE A. BREZINA,
ALLIED MEMBER, ASID**

Indonesia and the tropics merge in this inviting guest space. The muted ruby walls in the twin bedroom offer a comfortable, Asian-influenced space to relax. The light and airy quality of the coverlettes balance the space and introduce additional colors. The hand-painted papier-mache, wall-mounted Chinese robes are a part of the unusual accessories that complement the mood.

Photo credit: Nick Shirghio

Opposite

**ROMANZA INTERIOR DESIGN
MARNIE SORENSEN**

A guest suite of this proportion warrants the use of a commanding, four-poster bed. Warm tones of apricot, gold, and green provide a backdrop for this Mediterranean masterpiece. Bold stripes, muted plaids, and Asian-inspired lines create a calming solitude.

Photo credit: Laurence Taylor

GUEST ROOMS   43

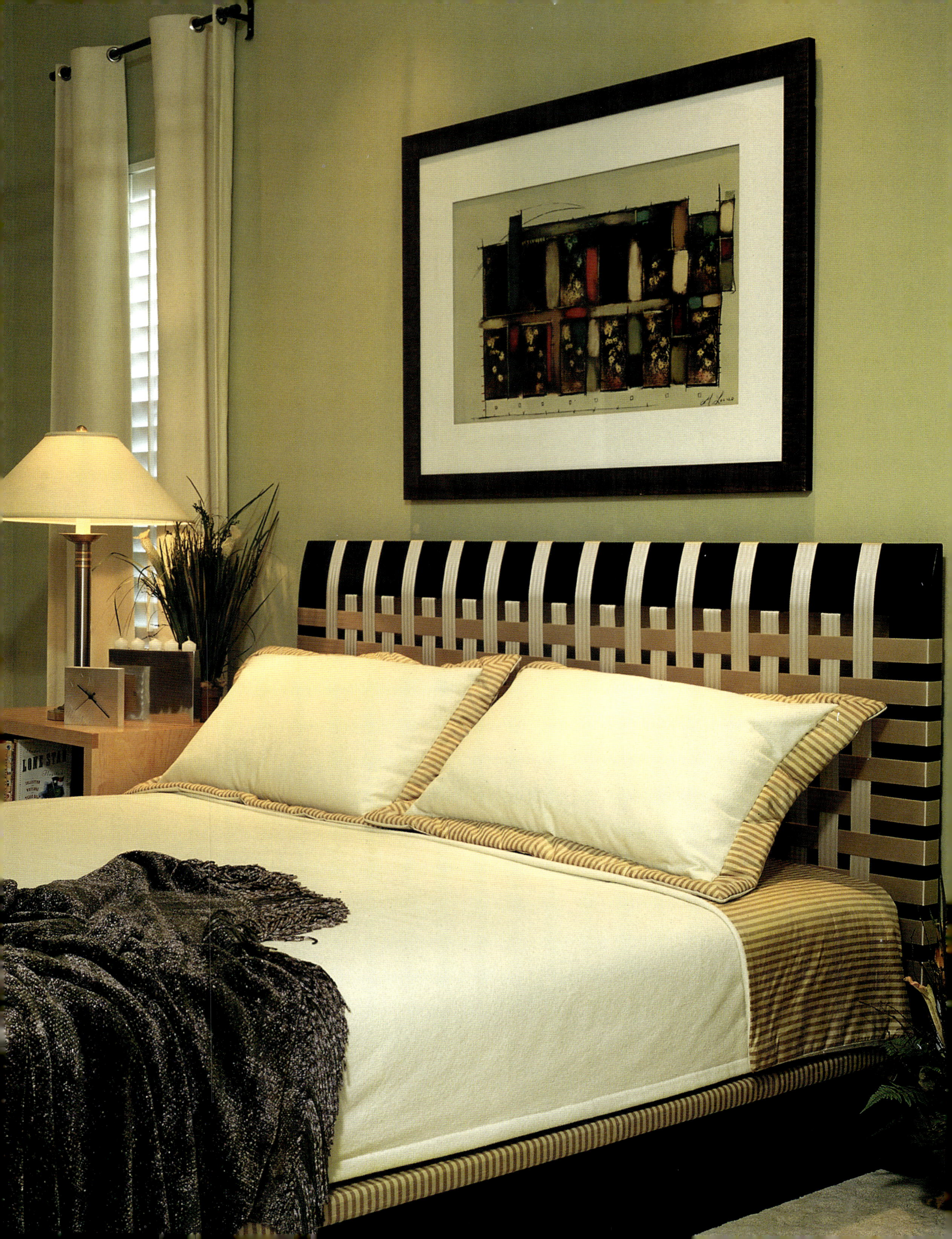
LONE STAR

Left

LINDY THOMAS INTERIORS
LINDY THOMAS, ASID

An incredible view is the only focal point this guest bedroom requires. The designers incorporated a soft yellow theme to maintain an interior that is as inspiring as the outside. A variety of textures keeps the color scheme interesting.

Below

ACCESSORIES ETC., INC.

The gold stripe, textured walls provide a comfortable background to the simple and uncluttered lines of this elegant black and gold self-contained bedroom suite. Niceties, including a morning bar and entertainment center, create a serene getaway for visitors. (*Builder: Frey & Son Homes*)

Photo credit: Jim Freeman

Opposite

K2 DESIGN GROUP, INC.

In this classic, modern guest room clean, sleek lines dominate the design. The shape of the custom-built, cypress headboard with contrasting webbing is showcased against the striking kiwi walls. An oil on canvas painting splashes deeper colors about, while neutral European shams and coverlet calm the scene.

GUEST ROOMS 45

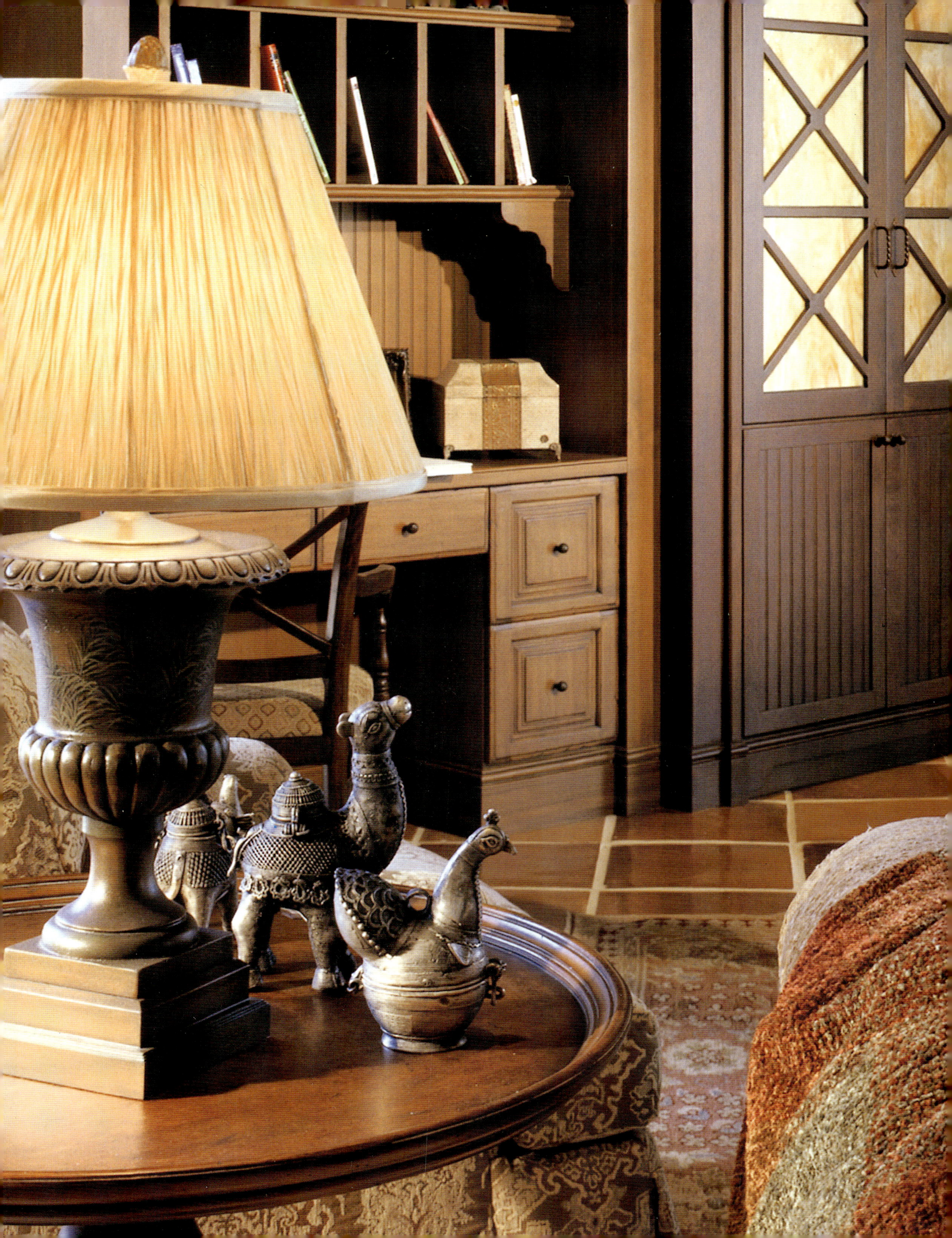

FAMILY ROOMS

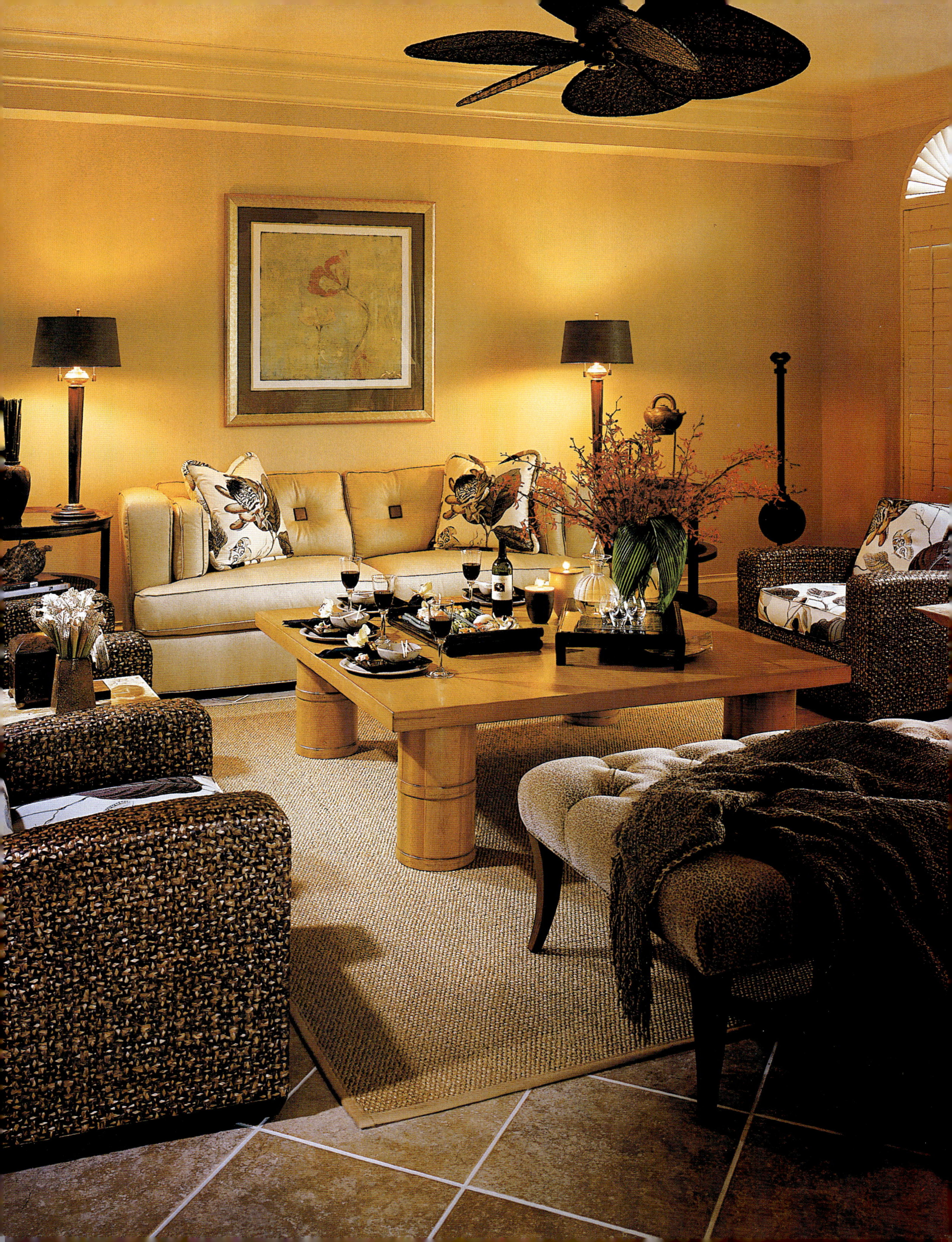

Left

VINCE MULLER INTERIOR
DESIGN, INC.
SUSAN JOSLIN-MULLER, ASID

A multitude of textures and rich spice tones create a comfortable West Indies-influenced design. A custom built-in utilizes three different wood finishes to lighten the mass of the piece. Mixed with stained and leaded glass panels, these wood tones blend well with the furnishings and fabrics in the room. The ceilings are tongue-and-groove cypress with hand-hewn wood beams. (*Builder, Hunt Construction*)

Photo credit: Joseph Lapeyra Photography

Below

ROBB & STUCKY
CYNDE THOMPSON, IDS, FLORIDA
LICENSED INTERIOR DESIGNER

This space utilizes an Olde Florida, Key West design concept to evoke a feeling of the island experience. Bamboo floors, woods, woven fibers, metals, raw silk pillows and panels all bring texture into the design. Woven wood cornices in tortoise, a hand-knotted Oriental rug, leather lamp shades, a seagrass cocktail table, and a deep maple finished armoire combine beautifully in this waterside retreat.

Photo credit: Jennifer Deane

Opposite

ROZ TRAVIS INTERIORS, INC.
ROZ TRAVIS

This downtown residence has an uptown appeal. A myriad of natural fibers and warm woods create a comfortable setting for gatherings prior to an evening of theater and strolling the avenue. Bold botanical prints add punch to the neutral tones and dark wood.

FAMILY ROOMS

Right

HOLLAND SALLEY
INTERIOR DESIGN
LESLIE CHRISTIAN, ASID, NCIDQ

The design concept incorporated in this living space is contemporary without being sterile, and combines many materials not typically used together. The use of fire, natural materials and water gives this unit a spiritually tranquil environment which reflects the views all around. The family room features highly lacquered wood veneers in the custom entertainment center, as well as furniture covered in natural textures and metal accents throughout.

Photo credit: Nick Shirghio

Below

DESIGN GROUP WEST
GLENN MIDNET, ASID, IDS

Use of color and texture make this room a tropical retreat. The color palette is a showcase of crisp reds, greens, golds and white. British West Indies-influenced mahogany wood furnishings and bamboo floors add warmth. Tropical Southwest Florida breezes flow through the residence from sliding glass doors, which usher the lanai and pool into the home. The liberal use of large palms and greenery further enhances the tranquil ambiance that invites one to relax and enjoy the moment.

Opposite

VALENTINE & STONE INTERIORS
MICHAEL VALENTINE, ASID &
ROBERTA VALENTINE

An eclectic assortment of accessories and furnishings complement the Mediterranean theme in this family room where a raised ceiling features a striped inset, giving a tent-like effect. The rich color palette of reds, purples, and greens complements the extensive architectural detail and varied faux finishes.

50 ~ FINE INTERIORS OF NAPLES, FLORIDA

FAMILY ROOMS 51

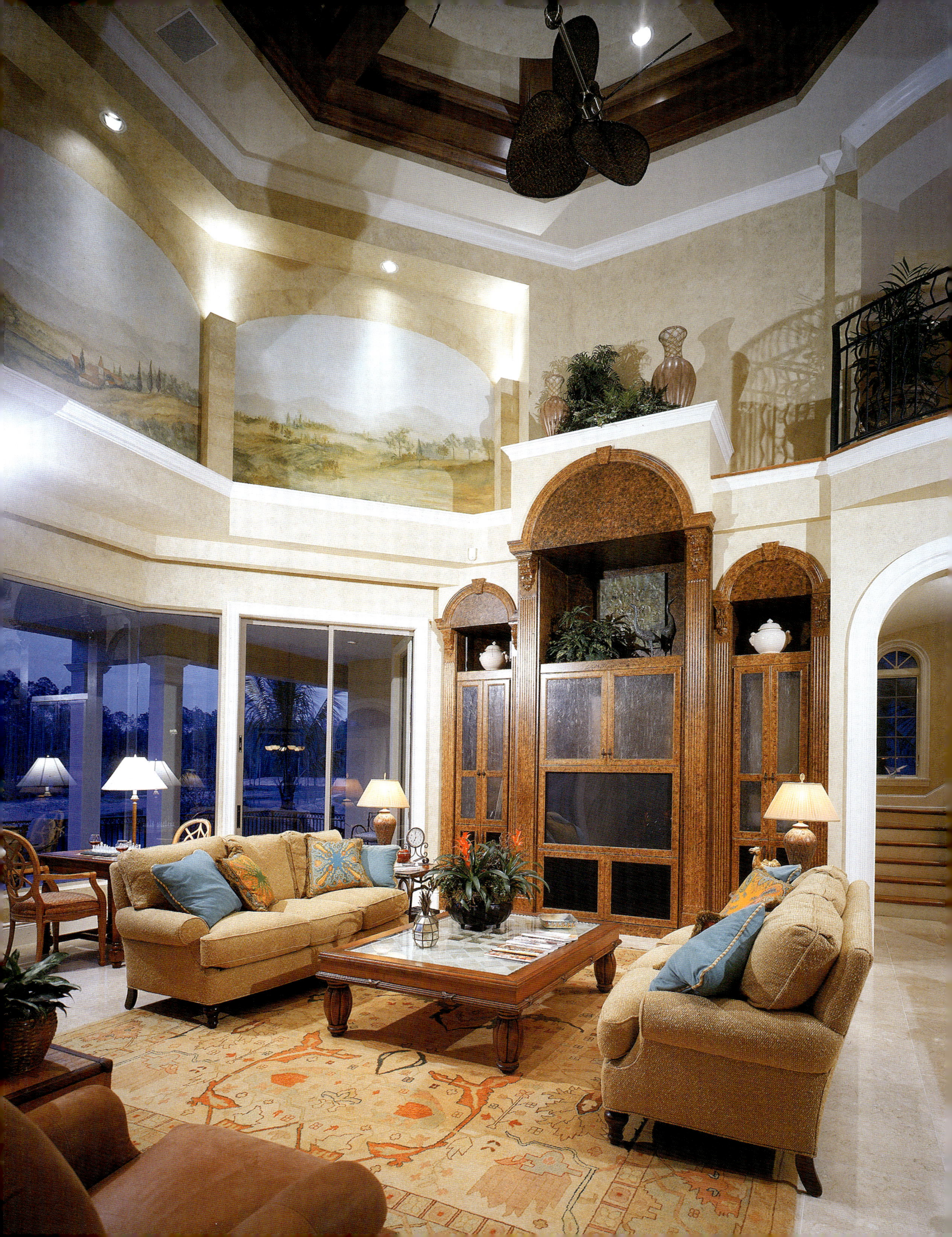

Left

ACCESSORIES ETC., INC.

A casual retreat inspired by nature is created in this room that features honey-toned wood paneling and a tongue-and-groove paneled ceiling with exposed beams. Overstuffed couches welcome visitors who are entertained by cutting-edge audio and visual technology. The floors created from reclaimed barn wood floors are carried through to the sunken bar and adjacent kitchen. (*Builder, Kurtz Homes*)

Photo credit: CJ Walker

Below

HOLLAND SALLEY
INTERIOR DESIGN
LINDA BURKE, ASID, NCIDQ

The den offers traditional elements which form a richly styled, comfortable interior and also provides a comfortable refuge. The room's function revolves around a hand-built, hand-finished desk/entertainment unit opposite a chenille sofa in camel.

Opposite

ACCESSORIES ETC., INC.

The colors of the Mediterranean—sand, burnt umber, terra cotta, and turquoise blue—are reflected in this family room. Despite the room's 26-foot ceilings, an intimate setting is created with beamed ceilings, rich, multi-layered crown moldings, art shelves, balconies and murals. With the simple lines of the twin sofas and custom-made table, the focus of the room becomes the grand, tortoise-finished, high-tech media center. (*Builder, Frey & Son Homes*)

Photo credit: Jim Freeman

FAMILY ROOMS   53

Right

DESIGN GROUP WEST
GLENN MIDNET, ASID, IDS

This room is accentuated with the flavor of Old World Italy. Such influences are evident in the intricate wrought iron and stone cocktail table, the richly hand-carved wood armoire with spiraling acanthus motif, and an oil painting hand-selected by the designer while in Milan. The colors are a relaxing and soothing palette of earth tones with a grounding punch of black to add sophistication. The walls are finished with a hand-applied Venetian plaster to add texture. A hand-tufted wool area rug finishes this room and anchors the cozy conversation area.

Left

ROBB & STUCKY
KELLI SMITH ASID, FLORIDA
LICENSED INTERIOR DESIGNER

This casual country club setting overlooking a golf course is ideal for entertaining. Designed to accommodate small gatherings, the family room utilizes a sisal area rug under the seating group that includes, two seagrass chairs, a carved cocktail table with glass inset, a chenille sofa, and linen chair. Raw silk window treatments and Saturnia floor complete the space.

Opposite

LUNDIN INTERIORS, INC.
RONALD E. LUNDIN, ALLIED
ASID, ASSOC, IIDA, ASSOC. IDS

A custom-designed rug with tropical leaves and flowers sets the stage for this eclectic room ideal for entertaining. Burlap glaze cornices with wrapped poles and side panels with greens and golds, frame a Florida tropical setting. Lizard chenille sofas and rattan chairs invite residents to relax and enjoy a good book or watch TV from this custom designed, built-in with scrolled iron accents.

FAMILY ROOMS 55

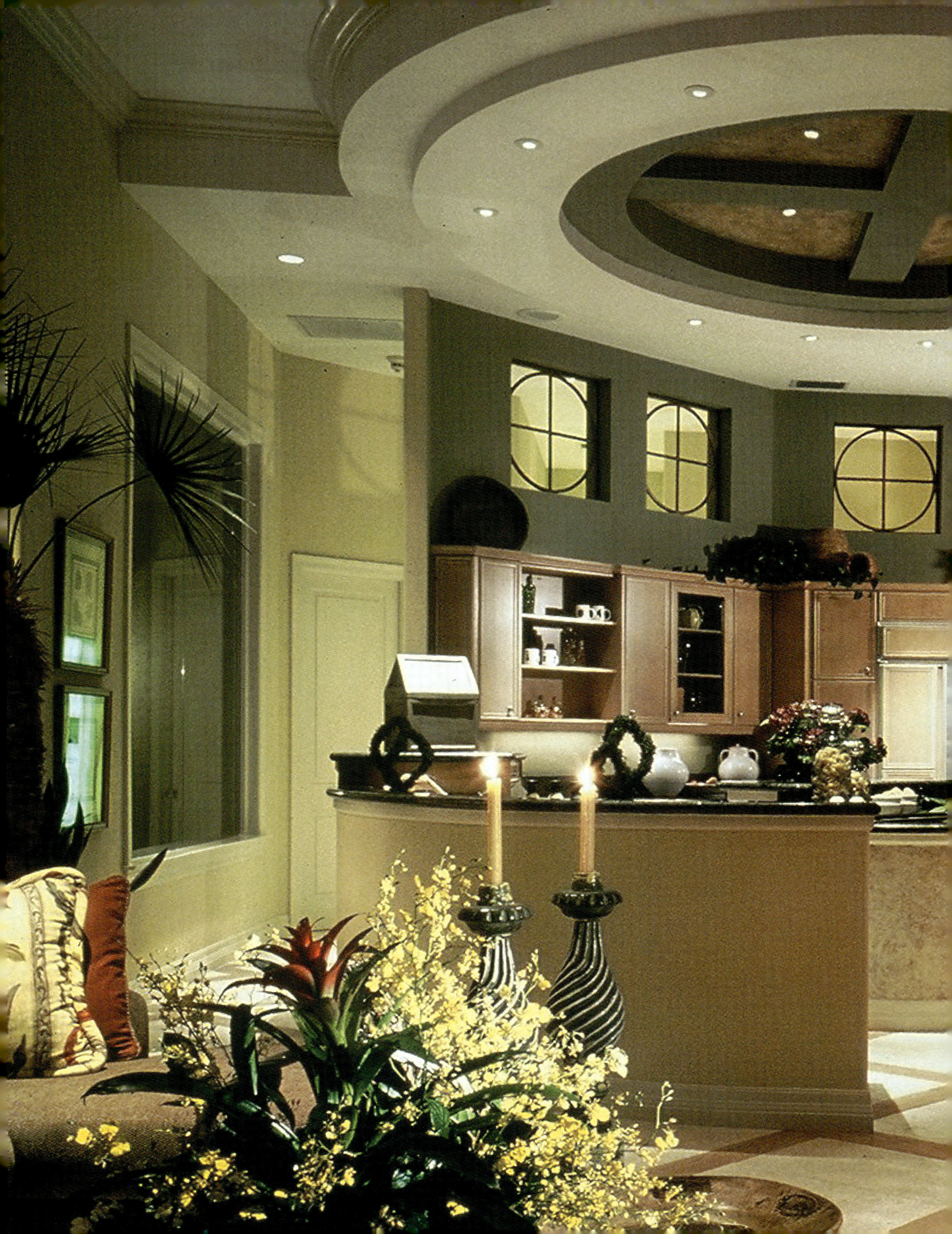

KITCHENS

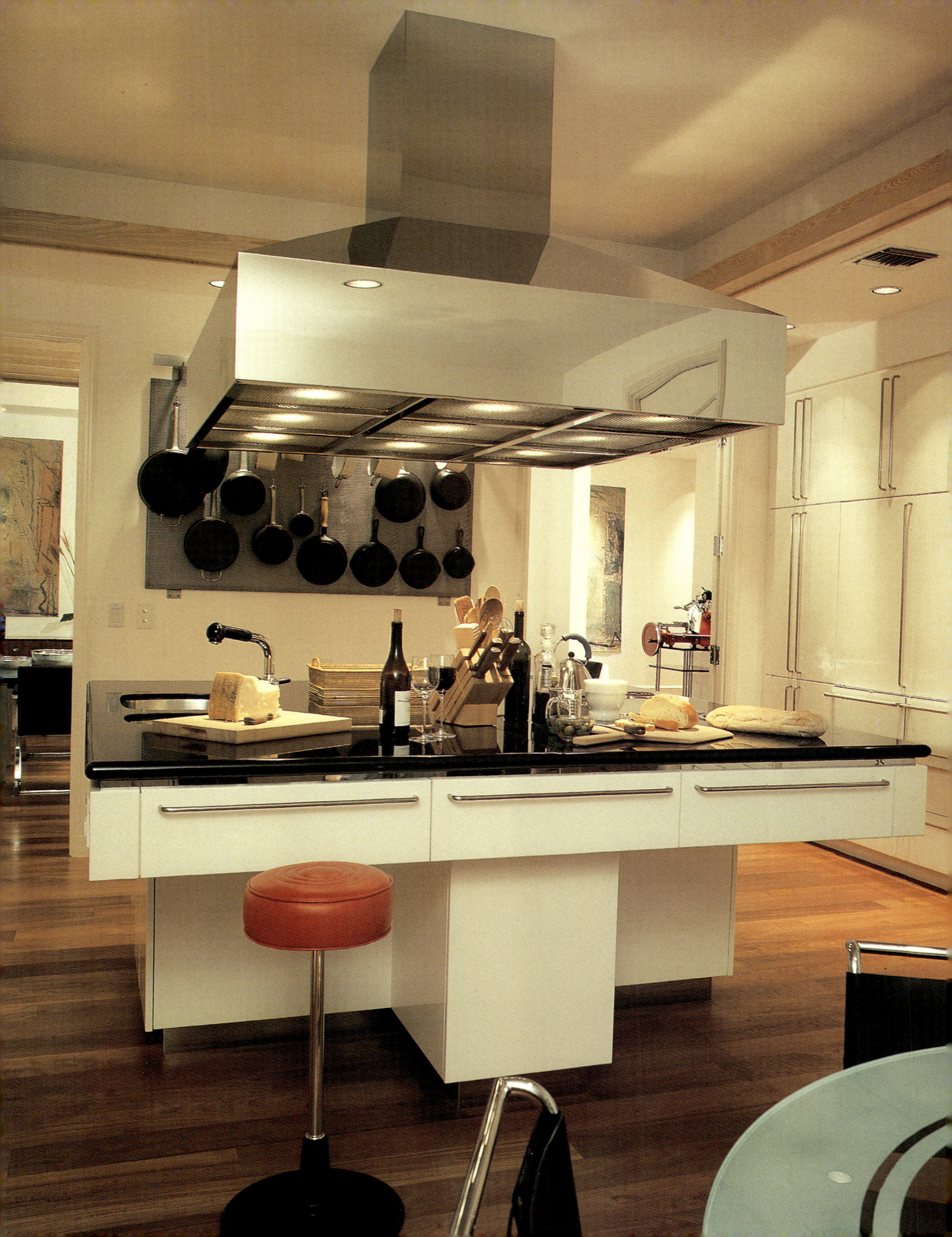

Left

K2 DESIGN GROUP, INC.
JENNY L. CARTER, ASID,
IIDA, ASSOC. AIA

This tropical, modern kitchen sports concentric circles. Although open to the great room area, it is very much its own space. Canadian-made cabinetry is segmented to follow the curved lines, and multi-level granite countertops gently separate work areas.

Photo credit: Laurence Taylor

Below

ROBB & STUCKY
KELLI SMITH, ASID, FLORIDA
LICENSED INTERIOR DESIGNER

This kitchen, inspired by Tuscany, is warm and inviting. The antique glazed cabinetry, granite countertops, and imported one-of-a-kind tumbled stone mosaic backsplash form the foundation for a rewarding culinary experience. Interesting details include an iron light fixture with crystals and a faux stone medallion over the stove.

Opposite

GEARY DESIGN, INC.
RICHARD F. GEARY III

In this modern kitchen, appliances and cabinetry seamlessly blend into the architecture, and the inner workings of the kitchen are hidden behind doors that open and pocket back to expose appliances and additional work surfaces. The seven-foot square island allows for ample preparation area and room for guests to gather round to assist or just watch. A small private breakfast area is in the kitchen space and the larger formal dining area for twelve is just through the doorway. Pots hang from a custom-designed rack for easy access, and the large custom stainless steel hood sheds plenty of light on the work surface and eliminates cooking odors.

Photo credit: Ed Chappell

KITCHENS 59

Right

GEARY DESIGN, INC.
RICHARD F. GEARY III

In this gourmet's delight there is always room for one more to work side-by-side at the black granite counters. A large center island allows several people to work at one time. The clean modern lines promote freedom of movement, and a chest-high, sculptured divider separates the kitchen from the formal dining area. Upper cabinets are replaced by a storage wall that runs down one entire side of the kitchen and appears as a decorative panel.

Photo credit: Ed Chappell

Below

LONDON BAY HOMES
PATRICIA WESLEY INTERIORS,
SAN JOSE, CA

This circular kitchen utilizes an open design. The flooring of tumbled, Hallan limestone is set in a four-piece, ashlar pattern. Accents of jade green tile insets with custom-cut tumbled limestone form a circular pattern. Custom designed cherry wood cabinetry and polished, verde, antique marble countertops engulf the space.

Photo credit: Laurence Taylor

Opposite

ROMANZA INTERIOR DESIGN
NATALIE SORENTINO

This kitchen features a large center work island containing a sink and two SubZero refrigerator drawers. Classic, light, cross-cut travertine flooring, cedar wood ceiling beams, countertops of honed limestone, and a center island countertop of ivory and gold dark granite warm the large space. A pot filler located above the range provides added convenience. All cabinetry is custom-made by Christopher Peacock. (*London Bay Homes*)

Photo credit: Laurence Taylor

FINE INTERIORS OF NAPLES, FLORIDA

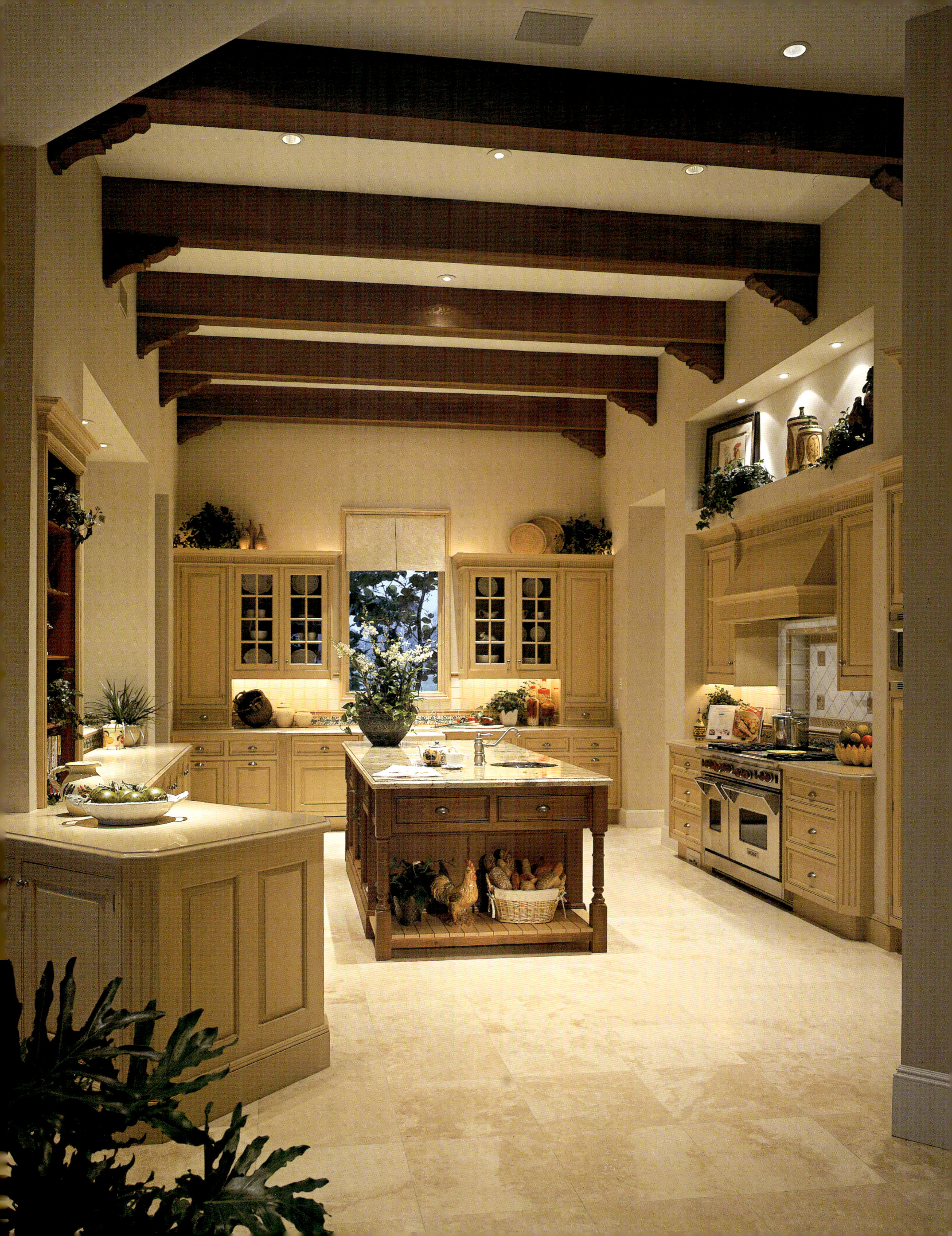

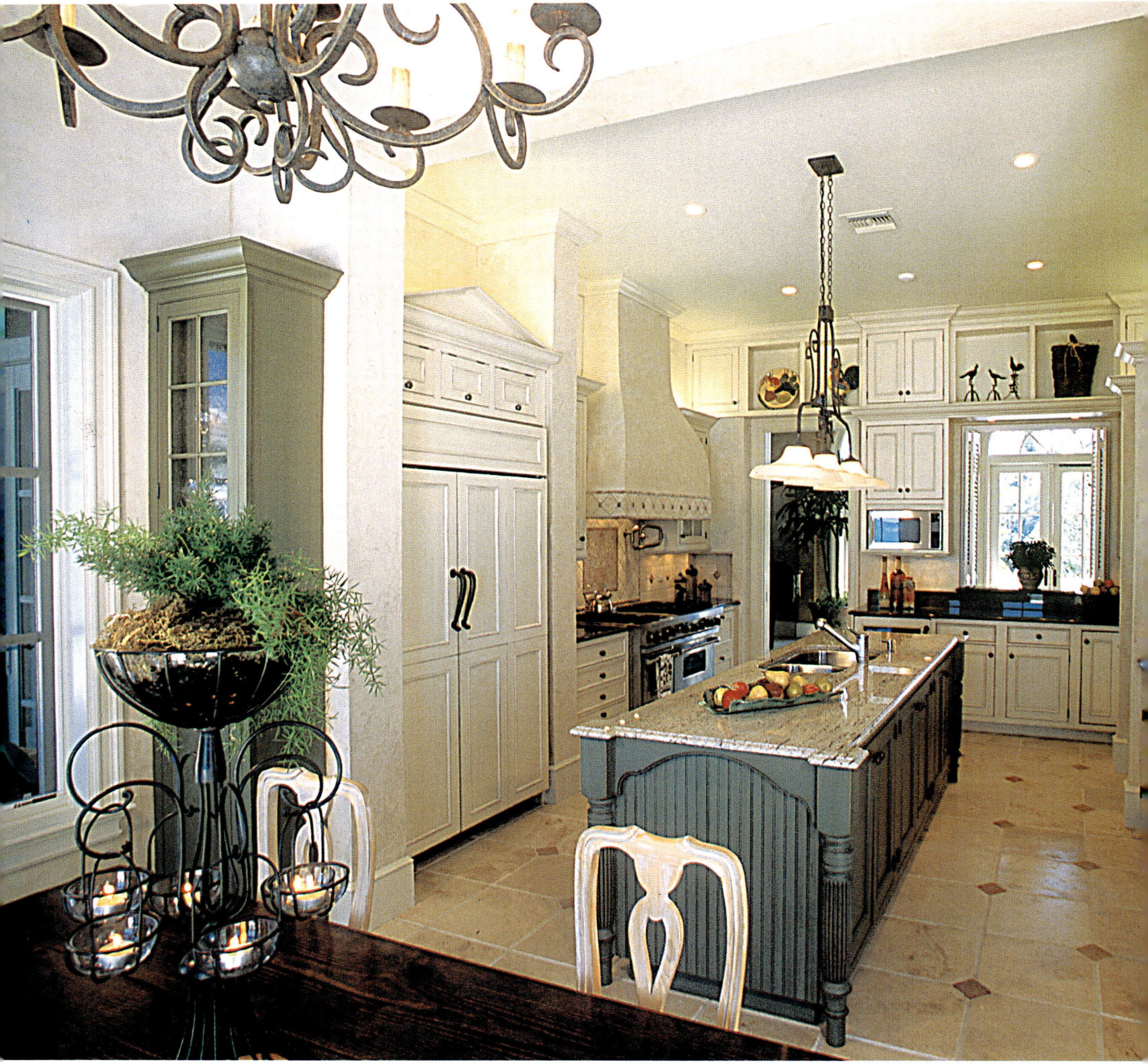

Left

PLATINUM COAST ARTISANS AND CRAFTSMEN

A farmhouse-style, country kitchen begins with warm wood floors and ends with a whimsical rooster. From the simple iron chandelier to the white kitchen cabinets antiqued with an oil glaze, this kitchen rings with comfort and familiarity. Display cabinets adjacent to the sink highlight sentimental pieces.

Below

THERESA CAROLLO INTERIORS
THERESA A. CAROLLO, ALLIED, ASID

This kitchen is the gathering place of the home. The cream-colored cabinets softly enhance the terra cotta and green mosaic tiles on the backsplash. A large center island in granite houses a sink and storage areas. The commercial stove/oven allows for a generous cooking area. The cast iron hood is fauxed in a Tuscany design and bordered in hand-painted Italian tiles. The kitchen overlooks the breakfast area and beautiful pool with landscaping.

Photo credit: Ron Blakeley

Opposite

DON EWY CONSTRUCTION

Painted cabinetry in olive and off-white create a farmhouse feel. The expansive island resembles a piece of furniture with its turned legs on the corners. Granite countertops, stone floors, and iron light fixtures reinforce the aged look in this functional space.

KITCHENS 63

Right

ACCESSORIES ETC., INC.

The perfect balance between form and function is achieved in this gourmet-styled kitchen. Fine furniture is combined with custom cabinetry to maximize storage. A light glaze added to the cabinetry creates a crisp, clean look against the dark wood and granite-topped, island work center. The tumbled marble in the backsplash, granite countertops and stone floors add to the appeal of an "all natural" kitchen.

Photo credit: Jim Freeman

Below

FREESTYLE INTERIORS
RAGAN HARRIS

Custom dark wood cabinetry and granite tops house gourmet appliances in this functional kitchen. A decorative center island with convenient veggie sink and a custom-designed hood set atop the mosaic backsplash provide plenty of workspace for a friendly group of chefs.

Opposite

HUNT CONSTRUCTION COMPANY, INC.
VINCE-MULLER INTERIOR DESIGN

Hand-hewn beam ceilings, granite countertops, and dark walnut finished cabinetry creates a rich, warm kitchen. The centerpiece of the hood is a beautiful tile mosaic which blends well with the wood tones throughout. Terracotta tiles are used on the floor as well as the backsplash of this unique kitchen.

Photo credit: Joseph Lapeyra Photography

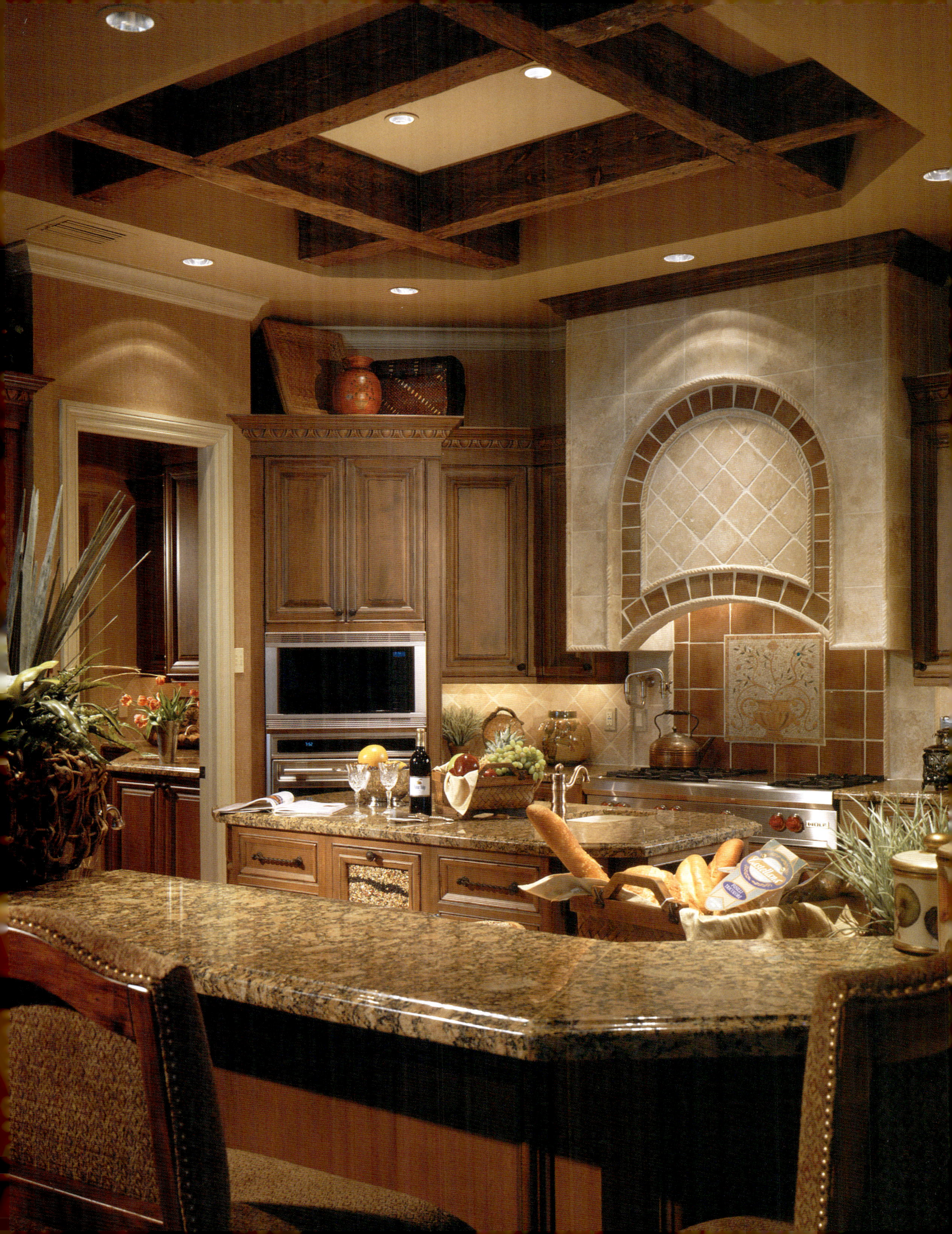

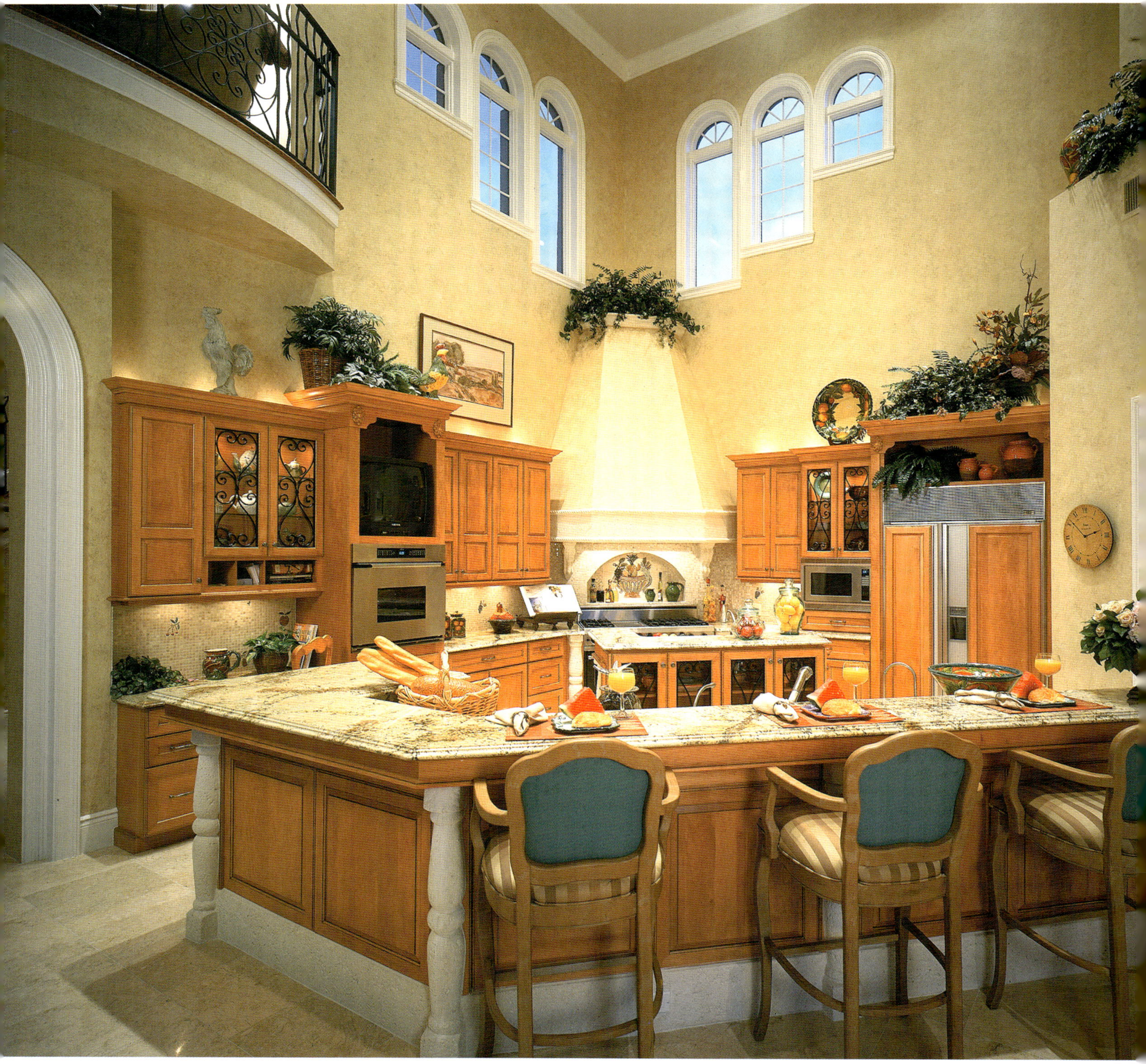

Left

**K2 DESIGN GROUP, INC.
JENNY L. CARTER, ASID, IIDA,
ASSOC. AIA**

Pearwood, maple and cherry contrast with stainless and anthracite grey lacquer in the kitchen of this designer's home. Black granite counters, although very practical, add drama. Modern furniture and equipment stand out against aged background of curry-colored, Venetian plaster.

Below

PLATINUM COAST ARTISANS AND CRAFTSMEN

A whimsical cottage-style home on the water is playful, light and airy. A specialty finish on the walls consists of a colorwash overlayed with a colorwash square pattern in white and turquoise. Lines of beadboard and simple stools reinforce the linear theme. Cool terra cotta tile and hand-painted chairs enhance the casual feel of the kitchen.

Opposite

ACCESSORIES ETC., INC.

A feast for all of the senses, this kitchen integrates an unusual combination of wood, keystone, granite and iron as complementary textures. The mosaic backsplash of polished marble with inserts of colored marble, creates a unique piece of dimensional art. Natural light from the stair-step windows floods the room. The gourmet, cooking center with stainless steel appliances and gas cooktop is an intimate space to create the cuisine de jour. (*Builder, Frey & Sons Homes*)

Photo credit: Jim Freeman

Right

NANCY HANNIGAN
FINE ART STUDIO
NANCY HANNIGAN, ARTIST

This hand-painted, custom design is one of many created for exclusive residences in Naples. A collection of fruits of the vine, orchard, and grove surround a fine vintage in this one-of-a-kind backsplash.

Below

ROMANZA INTERIOR DESIGN
JENNIFER STEVENS

The focal point in this culinary paradise is the range backsplash, which is an Italian, custom-designed creation featuring vibrant colored fruit and metallic silver marble accent tiles. Above the mosaic is a carved stone, range hood anchored by stone corbels. The Veneziano granite countertops contrast nicely with the butternut-stained cabinetry and antique pewter hardware. (*Builder, London Bay Homes*)

THERESA CAROLLO INTERIORS
THERESA A. CAROLLO,
ALLIED, ASID

The wine niche includes a Sub Zero controlled wine cooler. Hand-carved moldings crown the top of the cabinetry. Iron detailing at the top of the arch adds to the aura of the space. Light-hearted caricatures of the owners in a bistro setting add a sense of whimsy to the serious world of wine.

Photo credit: Ron Blakeley

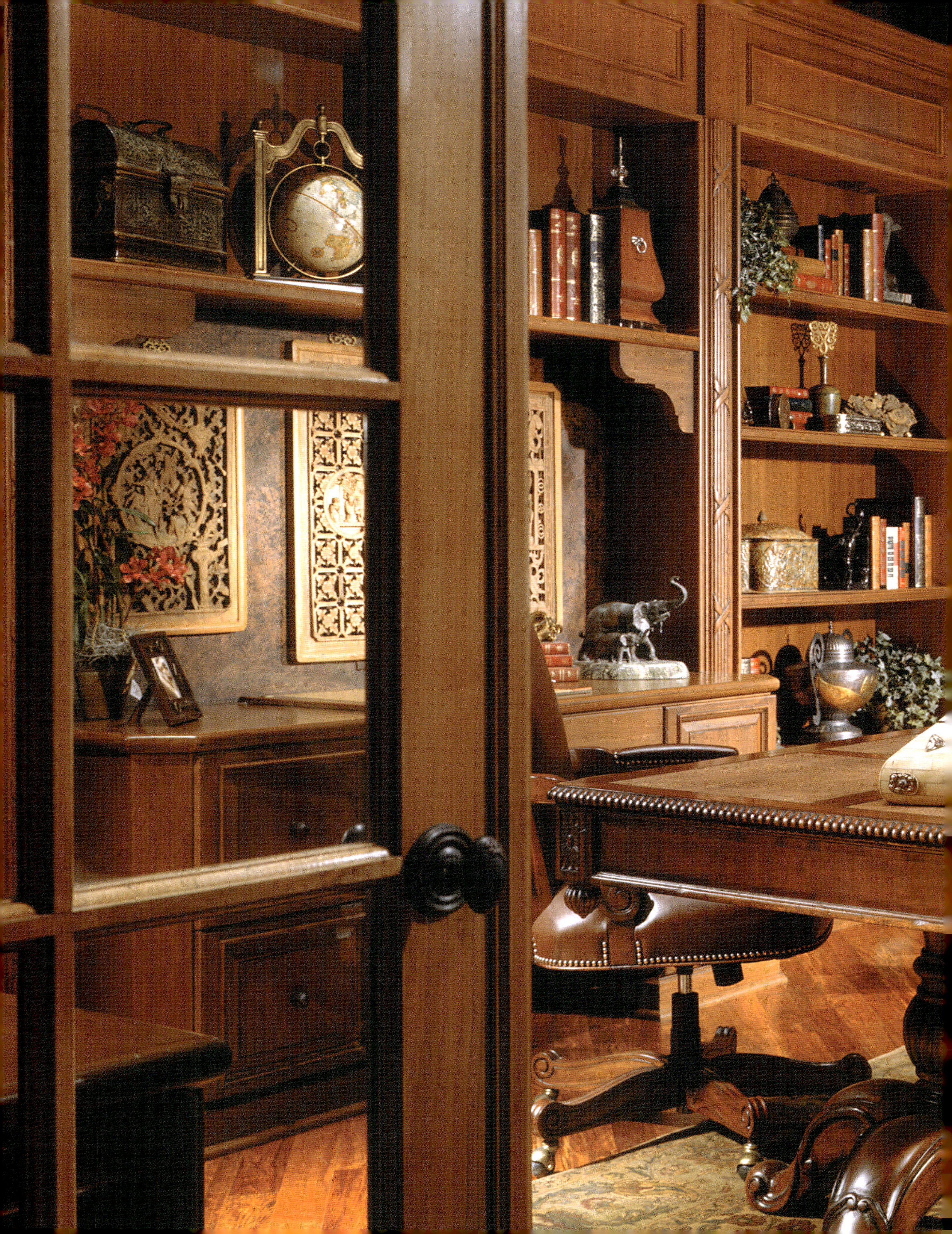

THE DEN

THE THOMAS RILEY ARTISANS' GUILD

This circular study is a custom-built design that artfully blends cherry with olive ash burl panels and hand-carved details with functional architectural elements. Art niches, bookcases and recessed panels surround the study with warmth and visual variety. Faux suede incorporated on the outer ceiling and a trompe l'oeil in the center ceiling offer a glimpse beyond the comfort of the room.

Above

THE THOMAS RILEY ARTISANS' GUILD

Equipped for several encore performances, this home theater incorporates classical elements with the comforts of 21st-century living. Geometric ceiling detail, recessed panels, and fluted columns on either side of the screen, are softened with flowing draperies and comfortable seating.

Right

HUNT CONSTRUCTION CO., INC.
VINCE-MULLER INTERIOR DESIGN

The various hues of the walnut floors appear throughout the study in the custom built-ins and stained wood moldings as well as the partner's desk with inset leather top. The Oriental rug softens the space while the textured faux finish adds depth. Oversized wood chairs with leather and chenille cushions provide comfort.

THE DEN 73

Right

K2 DESIGN GROUP, INC.
JENNY L. CARTER, ASID, IIDA, ASSOC. AIA

The study in this condominium is depicted as Euro Traditional with suede-finished walls and cherry and ebony millwork designed by K2. From the distinctive moldings to the Persian area rug, this retreat inspires reflection. Classic nailhead trim and executive leather imbue a rich, European feel.

Below

ACCESSORIES ETC., INC.

Sumptuous elegance is portrayed in this study. The richness and warmth of honey-toned wood paneling and the tongue-and-groove paneled ceiling with coffered beams provide a backdrop for the focal point—the gas fireplace surrounded by fluted columns, stately corbels, mantel, and granite. The luxuriant fabrics of the overstuffed chairs and Oriental area rug add softness and a soothing atmosphere. (*Builder, Kurtz Homes*)

Photo credit: CJ Walker

Opposite

ROMANZA INTERIOR DESIGN
JENNIFER STEVENS

A dramatic, two-story library is enveloped with custom maple cabinetry and built-ins atop teak flooring laid in a herringbone pattern with border accents of maple and walnut. The second-story reading loft is accessible via a spiral staircase. (*Builder, London Bay Homes*)

Photo credit: Laurence Taylor

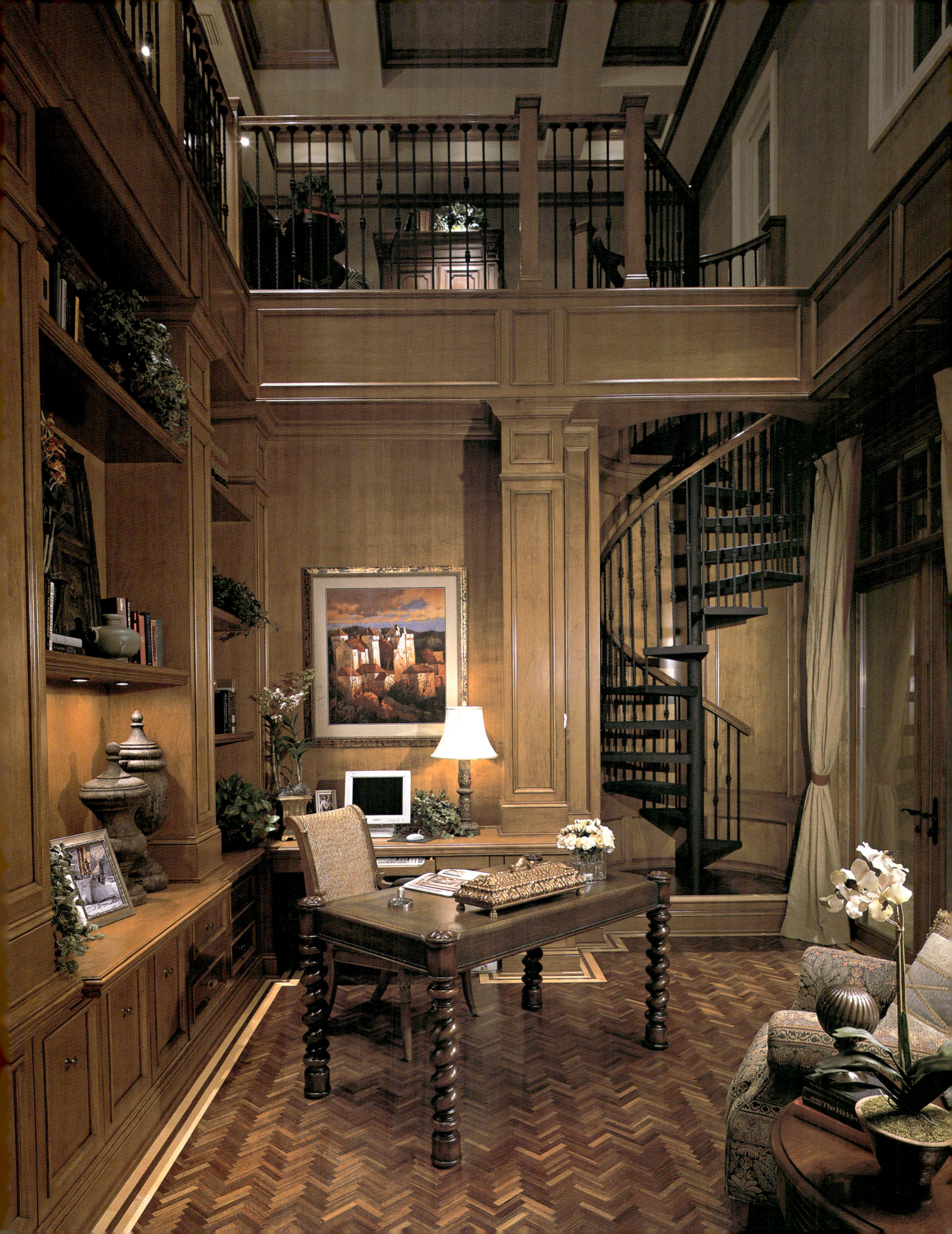

Right

**THERESA CAROLLO INTERIORS
THERESA A. CAROLLO,
ALLIED, ASID**

This gentleman's study displays a myriad of travel mementos. The herringbone-laid, chestnut stained, maple floor also appears as an accent in the coffered ceiling, creating a dramatic effect. A textured, green grasscloth and an environmentally protected zebra rug add character to this comfortable retreat. In addition, the chandelier with amber beaded shades offers warmth to the room. Functional elements include chestnut-stained custom cabinetry with bookcases, a computer credenza, and a kidney-shaped desk with leather inset.

Photo credit: C.J. Walker

Below

**JINX MCDONALD DESIGNS, INC.
JINX MCDONALD, IDS, ASID**

The coziness of this den emanates from the warm and interesting mixture of textiles. Water hyacinth, seagrass, bamboo and leather all create an inviting, tropical atmosphere.

Opposite

**ROBB & STUCKY
CHRISTINE ARNOLD, ASID,
FLORIDA LICENSED
INTERIOR DESIGNER**

Rich, wood tones and cream walls promote a masculine yet casual setting and a bit of a contrast to a traditional Florida office. Animal prints incorporated subtly in the design, a library ladder, and a brown cherry desk with burl wood lend a European library feel to this eclectic design.

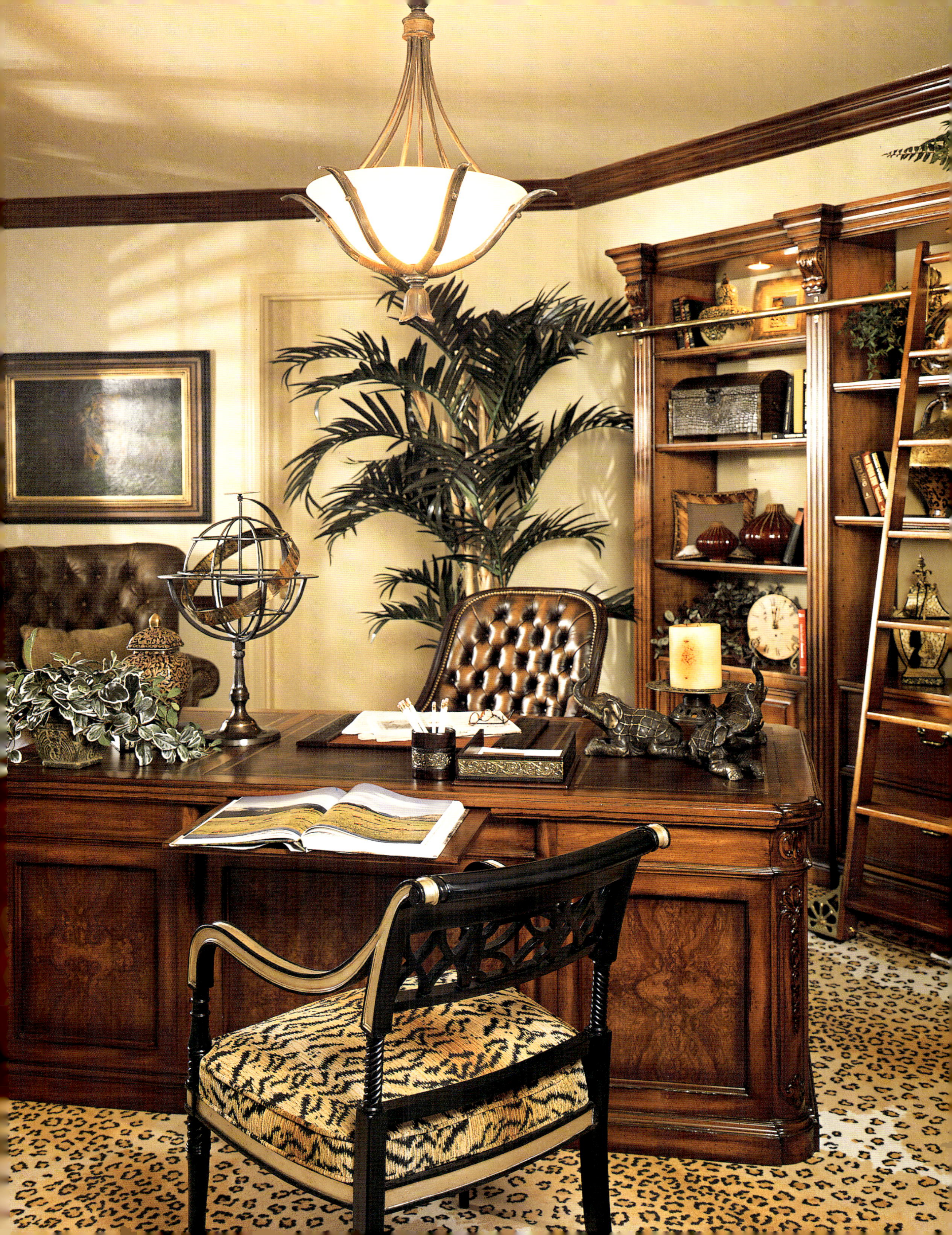

Left

ACCESSORIES ETC., INC.

Sumptuous textures and rich tones create a dramatic, in-home office. The walls are upholstered in suede with brass tacks. The tapestry-upholstered chair and coordinating window treatment add warmth to the sleek, custom-designed work center. (*Builder: Frey & Son Homes*)

Photo credit: Jim Freeman

Opposite

ROMANZA INTERIOR DESIGN
NATALIE SORRENTINO

Arches and decorative iron railings draw attention to the reading loft on the second floor of the library, which is accessible via private elevator. Warm maple wood trim and custom, maple built-ins are accented by the muted color wash on the faux finished walls. The Lapacho wood, commonly known as Brazilian walnut, floors further enhance the contemplative mood of the library. (*Builder, London Bay Homes*)

Photo credit: Laurence Taylor

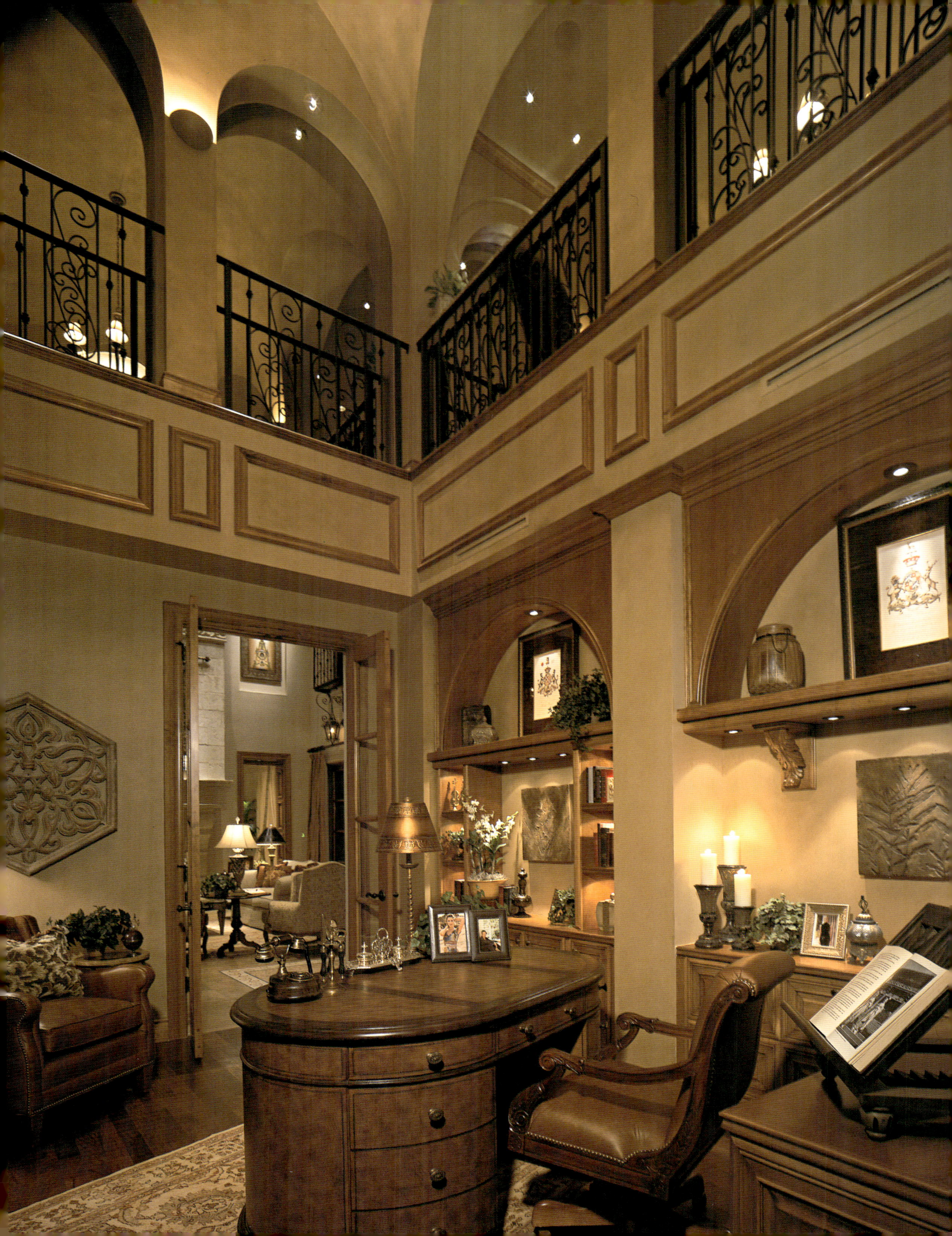

Right

LINDY THOMAS INTERIORS
LINDY THOMAS, ASID

An updated and sophisticated interpretation of British Colonial styling equates to a civilized setting for work and quiet contemplation. The architectural drama of the ceiling is enhanced by the subdued color palette of the room. Antiques and clean-lined furnishings actualize a very refined space for study.

Photo credit: Greg Wilson

Below

LINDY THOMAS INTERIORS
LINDY THOMAS, ASID

This beautiful setting is arranged on a Saturnia floor with black slate accent corners, adding a formal touch to a cottage on the water. The rattan chairs promise leisurely sitting while surrounded with antiquities like the casual table and Italian floor lamp.

Photo credit: Oscar Thompson

Opposite

THE THOMAS RILEY
ARTISANS' GUILD
ROMANZA INTERIOR DESIGN

Classy and refined, this lady's office is a testament to superior woodworking. Fabricated of American maple with maple burl inset panels, the built-in cabinetry beautifully combines form with function; even the air conditioning ducts are integrated into the open shelves. The design includes rosettes, frieze boards and dramatic corbels, all carved by hand and artistically finished in elegant gold and silver leaf. The blond finish reflects the light and airy atmosphere that makes this workspace comfortable for any task.

Photo credit: Laurence Taylor

80   FINE INTERIORS OF NAPLES, FLORIDA

THE DEN 81

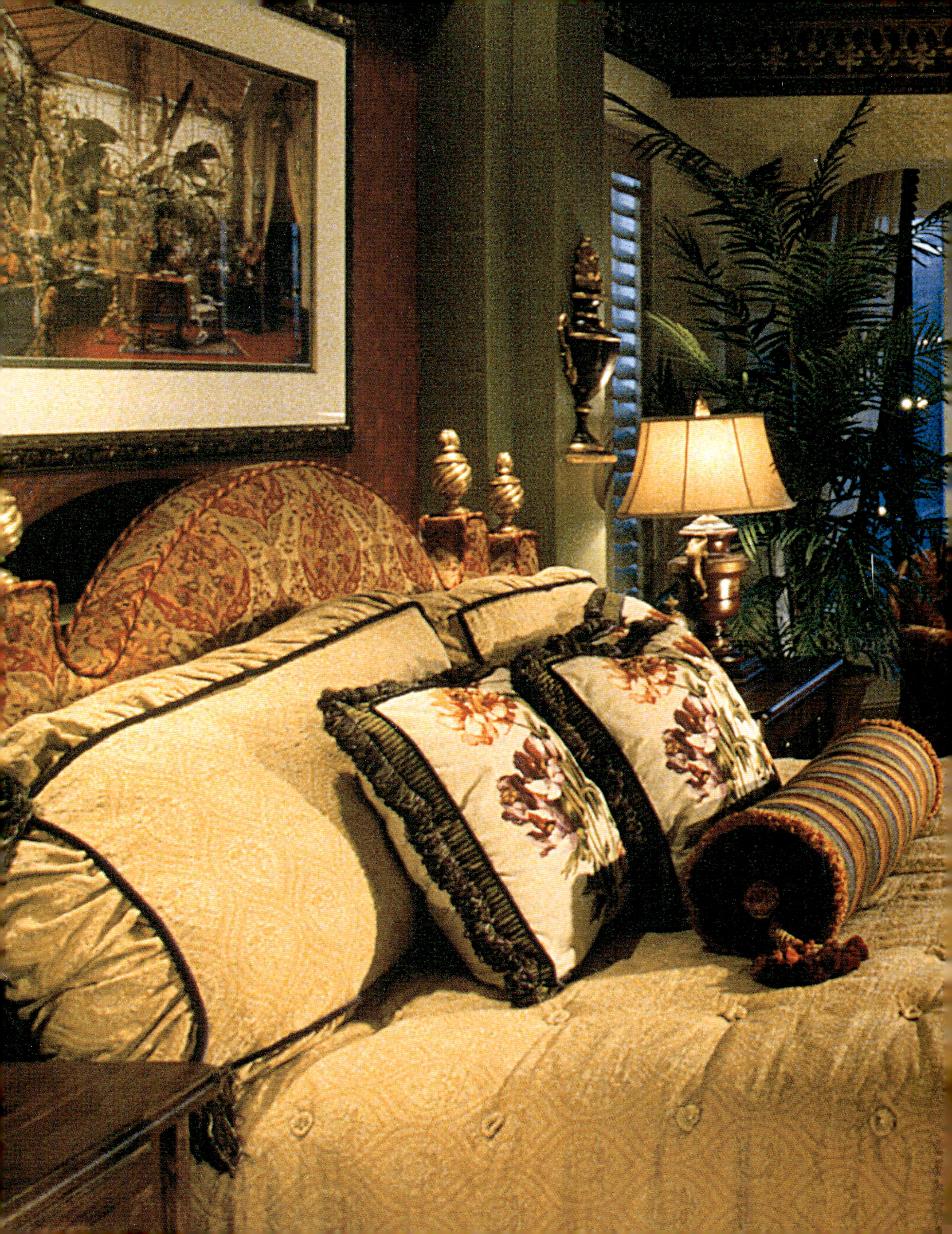

MASTER BEDROOMS

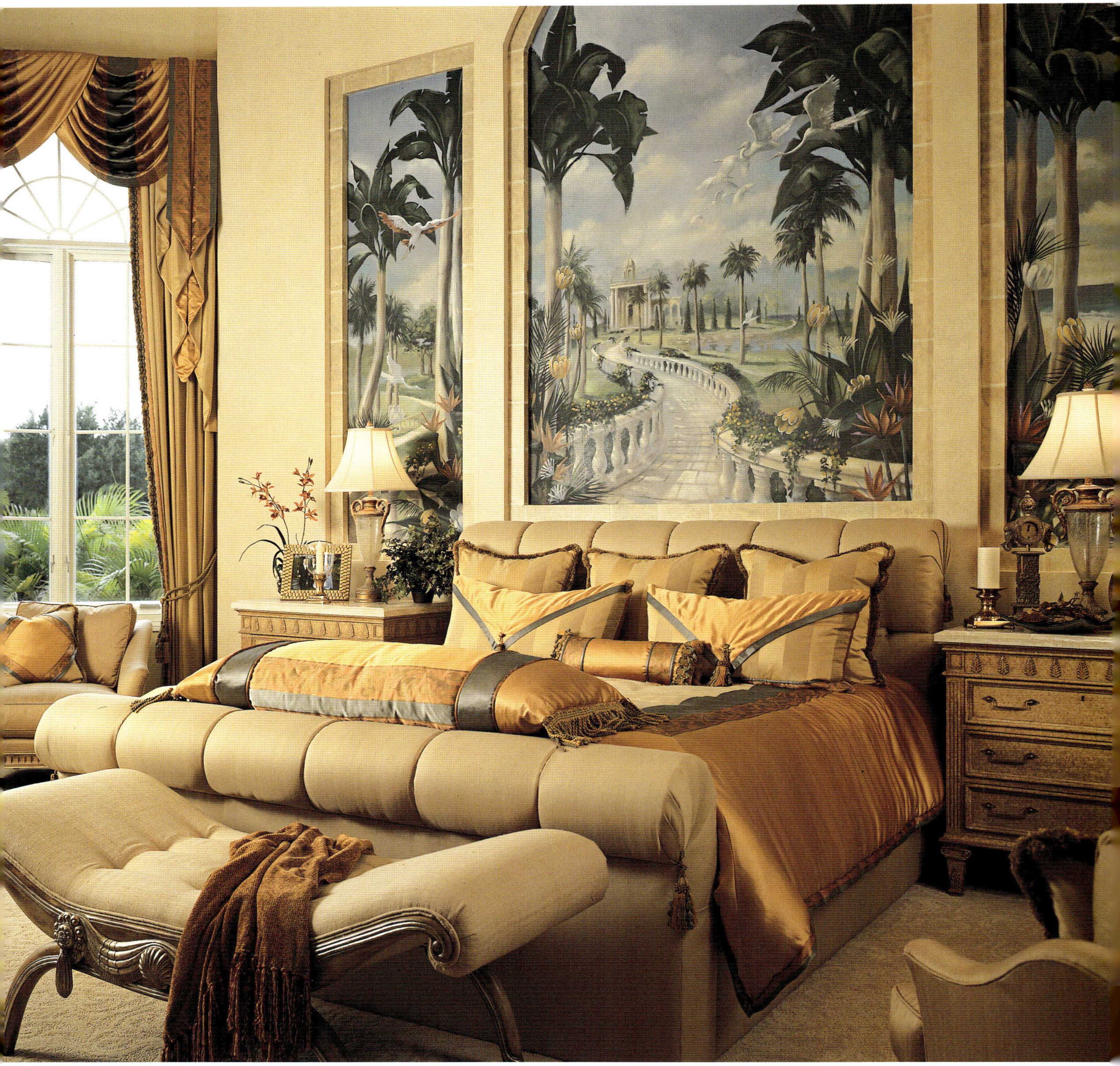

Left

HOLLAND SALLEY INTERIOR DESIGN
LESLIE CHRISTIAN, ASID, NCIDQ

The master suite of this sleek, contemporary unit offers a calm, serene refuge. The design concept is contemporary without being sterile and combines many materials that are not typically used together. Although the materials are dark and organic, the warm and inviting ambience is reflected in the copper tones of the leather padded headboard and footboard of the magnificent, king-size bed.

Photo credit: Nick Shirghio

Below

VALENTINE & STONE INTERIORS
MICHAEL VALENTINE, ASID AND ROBERTA VALENTINE

This dramatic master suite features a custom headboard with gold leaf finials, highlighted by the alcove built above the bed. The ceiling with gold, tealeaf insets and double borders creates a sense of drama. The designer's attention to detail is exemplified by the utilization of bouffettes on the coverlets and Turkish pillow shams with rushing and tassels.

Opposite

LUNDIN INTERIORS
RONALD E. LUNDIN, ALLIED ASID, ASSOC, IIDA, ASSOC. IDS

This beautiful master suite is engulfed by a whimsical Olde Florida mural, which brings the outdoors in with lush tropical birds and foliage. Custom silk draperies and bedding in golds, corals, and blues create an elegant retreat.

MASTER BEDROOMS

Right

**THERESA CAROLLO INTERIORS
THERESA A. CAROLLO,
ALLIED ASID**

A carved wood headboard with silk upholstery is set into a faux finished niche. The fabrics of chenille and silk in gold, brown, green and cream add luxury to the suite. Custom wood spiral poles, finished in gold, hold silk draperies and fringe to create a luxurious environment.

Photo credit: Ron Blakeley

Below

**K2 DESIGN GROUP, INC.
JENNY L. CARTER, ASID,
IIDA, ASSOC. AIA**

The walls in this master bedroom appear aged due to a colorwash technique applied with cheesecloth. The leather bed by Matteo Grassi combines rigidity with softness with an unmistakably modern design. Novosuede draperies in broad horizontal stripes and original artwork by Russian and American artists complement the Italian Modern space.

Photo credit: Oscar Thompson

Opposite

**ROBB & STUCKY
BETTI WALCOTT, ASID, IDS,
FLORIDA LICENSED
INTERIOR DESIGNER**

Opulence is reflected in every aspect of this Olde World, elegant master bedroom. Formal surroundings include a metal, four-poster, canopied bed where bed draperies can completely enclose the occupants. An elevated, private seating area is framed with lush, silk draperies.

FINE INTERIORS OF NAPLES, FLORIDA

MASTER BEDROOMS 87

88   FINE INTERIORS OF NAPLES, FLORIDA

Left

**VINCE MULLER INTERIOR DESIGN, INC.
KELLI VINCE, ASID**

The upholstered headboard in a red chenille fabric creates a very dramatic statement in this master bedroom. The recessed niche behind the bed, with the custom stone columns and hand-made wallcovering, adds dimension and softness to the space. (*Builder, McGarney Custom Homes*)

Photo credit: Thompson Harper Photography

Below

ACCESSORIES ETC., INC.

This master suite is a perfect retreat. The soft tone of the hand-painted, Tuscan hillside mural is the central focus of the master suite niche. The bed coverings are accented by a Fortuny-style print in cream and soft blue hues. The adjacent sitting room is surrounded by large windows, the perfect spot for a reflective moment. (*Builder, Frey & Son Homes*)

Photo credit: Jim Freeman

Opposite

**COLLINS & DUPONT INTERIORS, INC.
SHERRON P. DUPONT, ASID**

Mediterranean styling with a strong Spanish influence is reflected in this seductive master suite. Underfoot, Mexican clay tiles combine with chestnut flooring to set the stage for the metal, four-poster bed and raised sitting area. Convenience is cloaked with sophistication in the built-in vanity with antiqued, leaded mirror.

Photo credit: Laurence Taylor

MASTER BEDROOMS

Right

JINX MCDONALD DESIGNS, INC.
JINX MCDONALD, IDS, ASID

This master bedroom, while elegant, has a very casual and inviting ambiance. The colors are light and soft, and the furnishings speak of comfort and practicality.

Below

THERESA CAROLLO INTERIORS
THERESA A. CAROLLO,
ALLIED ASID

This master suite is a luxurious getaway with its soft fauxed walls in silver, cream, and gold accents. The four-poster bed is fit for the king and queen of the home. A separate sitting area with breakfast bar and overstuffed chairs allows for reading and quiet time.

Photo credit: Ron Blakeley

Opposite

VALENTINE & STONE INTERIORS
MICHAEL VALENTINE, ASID &
ROBERTA VALENTINE

A color palette of neutral tones of gold, with purple and green accents, provides a dramatic background for this master bedroom suite. The headboard was created by laminating fabric to the inside of an alcove, which is framed with accent painted moldings. Artwork is displayed in niches, highlighted with contrast color. A tropical ambiance is established with leaf-patterned wallpaper in the alcove and palm leaves and Macaws on the lamps.

FINE INTERIORS OF NAPLES, FLORIDA

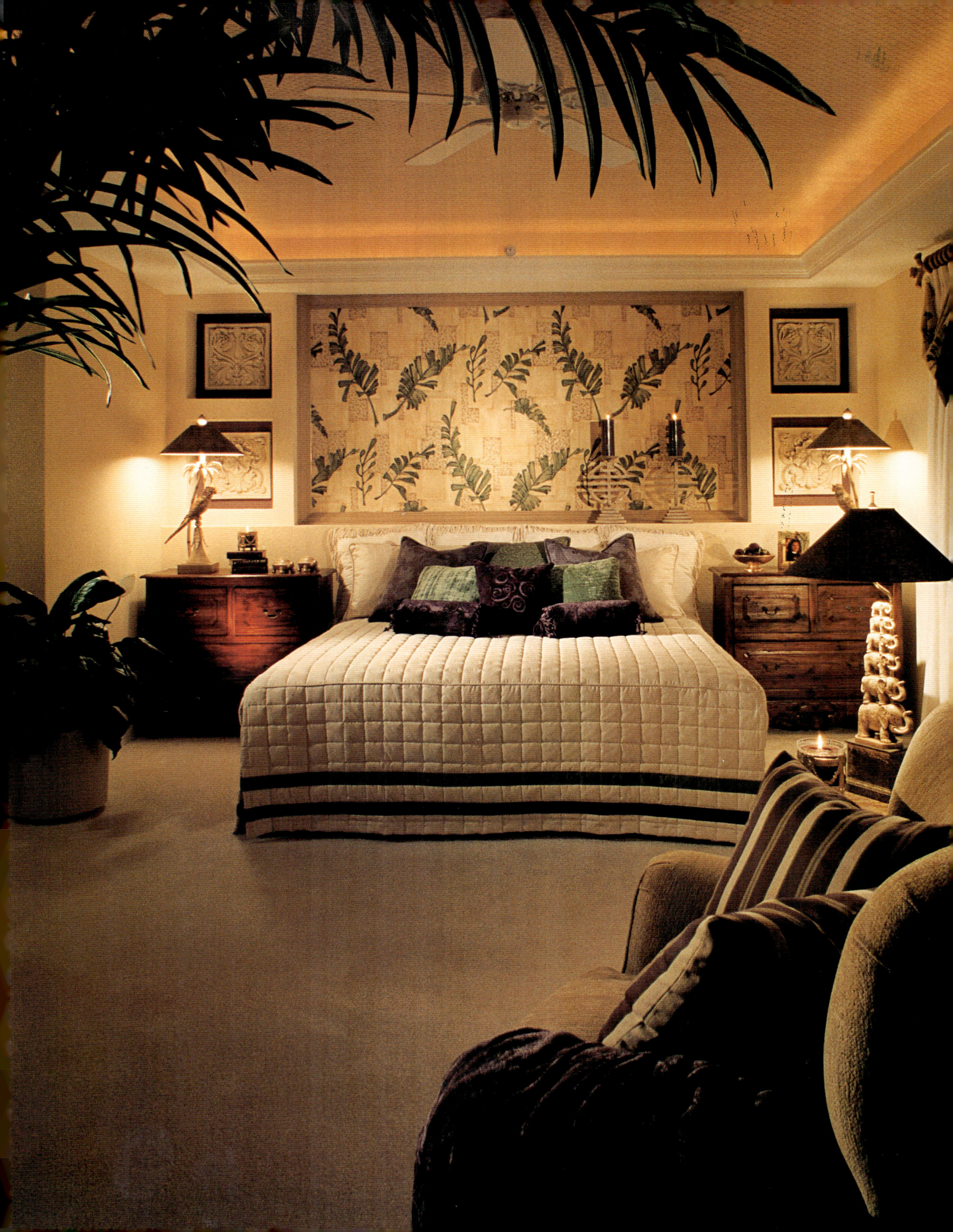

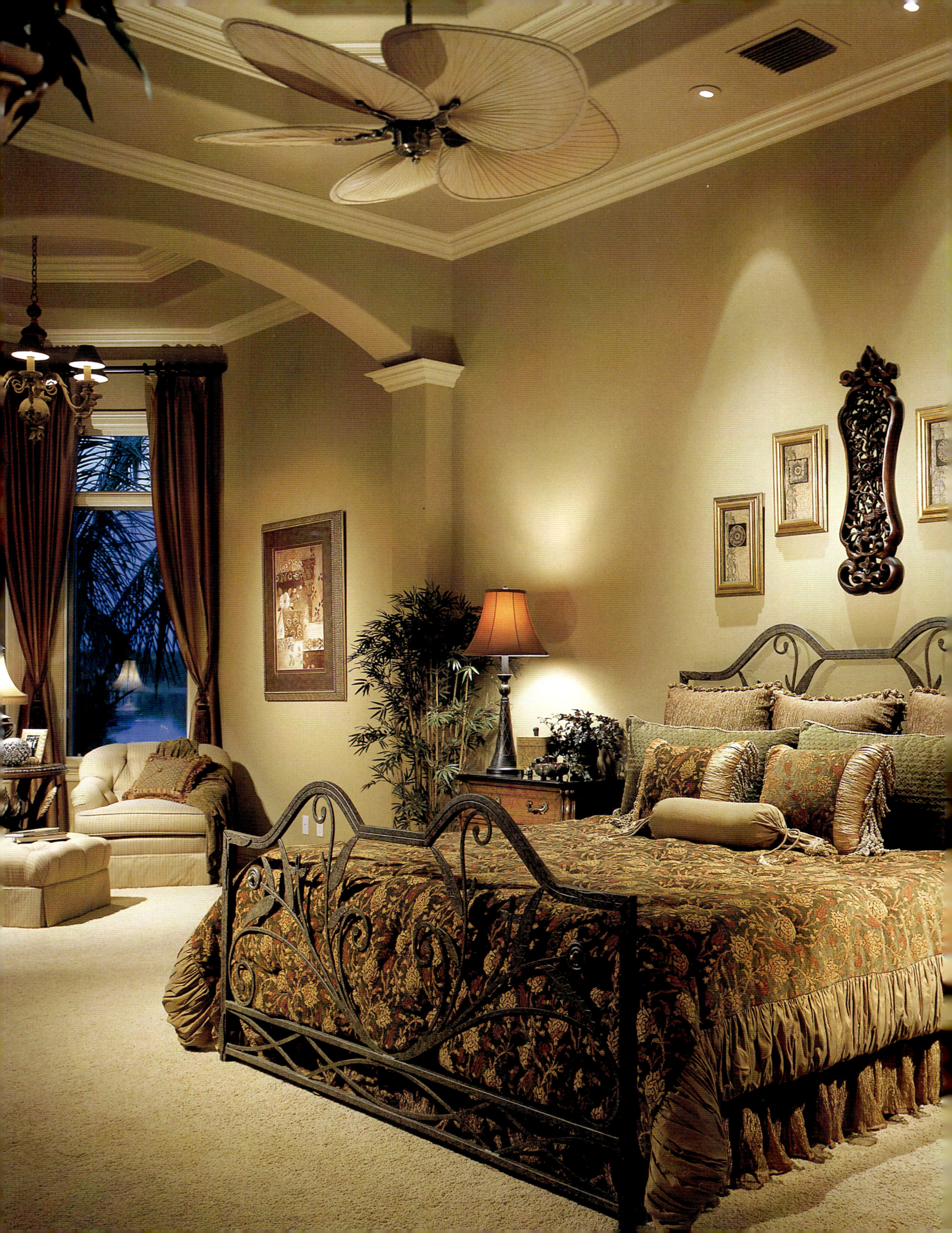

Left

HUNT CONSTRUCTION CO., INC.
VINCE-MULLER
INTERIOR DESIGN

Decadently cozy, this master suite includes a large sitting area with a three-sided fireplace that serves as a dramatic focal point. The distressed leather headboard and footboard embrace the quilted cranberry and gold duvet along with the floral silk detailing, and leather and velvet pillows.

Photo credit: Joseph Lapeyra Photography

Below

ROZ TRAVIS INTERIORS
ROZ TRAVIS

Uptown sophistication reigns in this clean and crisp master bedroom near 5th Avenue South. A luscious persimmon hue creates the backdrop for a contemporary headboard design. Adorned with sumptuous bedding and silk accent pillows in cinnabar and mocha, this bedroom melds traditional with modern.

Opposite

VINCE MULLER
INTERIOR DESIGN
DENISE WARD, ASID

Featuring a hand-forged, wrought iron bed and a quilted tapestry spread combined with rich silks, this master bedroom is an invitingly elegant, yet comfortable retreat. The palm frond ceiling fan and dark wood accents lend a formalized West Indies flair. (*Builder, Hunt Construction*)

Photo credit: Joseph Lapeyra Photography

Right

HOLLAND SALLEY
INERIOR DESIGN
LESLIE CHRISTIAN, ASID, NCIDQ

A contemporary style penthouse on the beach is quite unusual in Naples. Design concepts from the 1920s, mixed with a desire for warm and comfortable surroundings, create the foundation for this bedroom. Fabric textures, neutral tones with strong primary accents, and custom furniture created by the designer all combine to add warmth. The natural fiber-woven bed frame evokes an organic feel, yet does not distract from the contemporary theme of the penthouse.

Photo credit: Ed Chappell

Below

GEARY DESIGN, INC.
RICHARD F. GEARY III

This master bedroom offers a view of the peaceful garden and pool area. Muted tones complement the natural surroundings, while the fully upholstered, custom designed bed and classic Le Courbusier lounge offer the owners options for reading and relaxing. The Paul Manes painting carries the same tones, and the corner window allows plenty of natural light. The custom designed desk conceals a computer, and the Tansu chests complete the blending of traditional and contemporary.

Photo credit: Dan Forer

Opposite

K2 DESIGN GROUP, INC.
JENNY L. CARTER, ASID, IIDA, ASSOC. AIA

This bedroom reflects a combination of tropical, modern, and Zen-like qualities. An alcove with a built-in headboard and night tables solves a space problem. The cast medallions above the bed, typically used as exterior applications, feel right at home as interior design elements. Limited use of pattern and color allows form to be the prime element.

Photo credit: CJ Walker

MASTER BEDROOMS 95

M

MASTER BATH

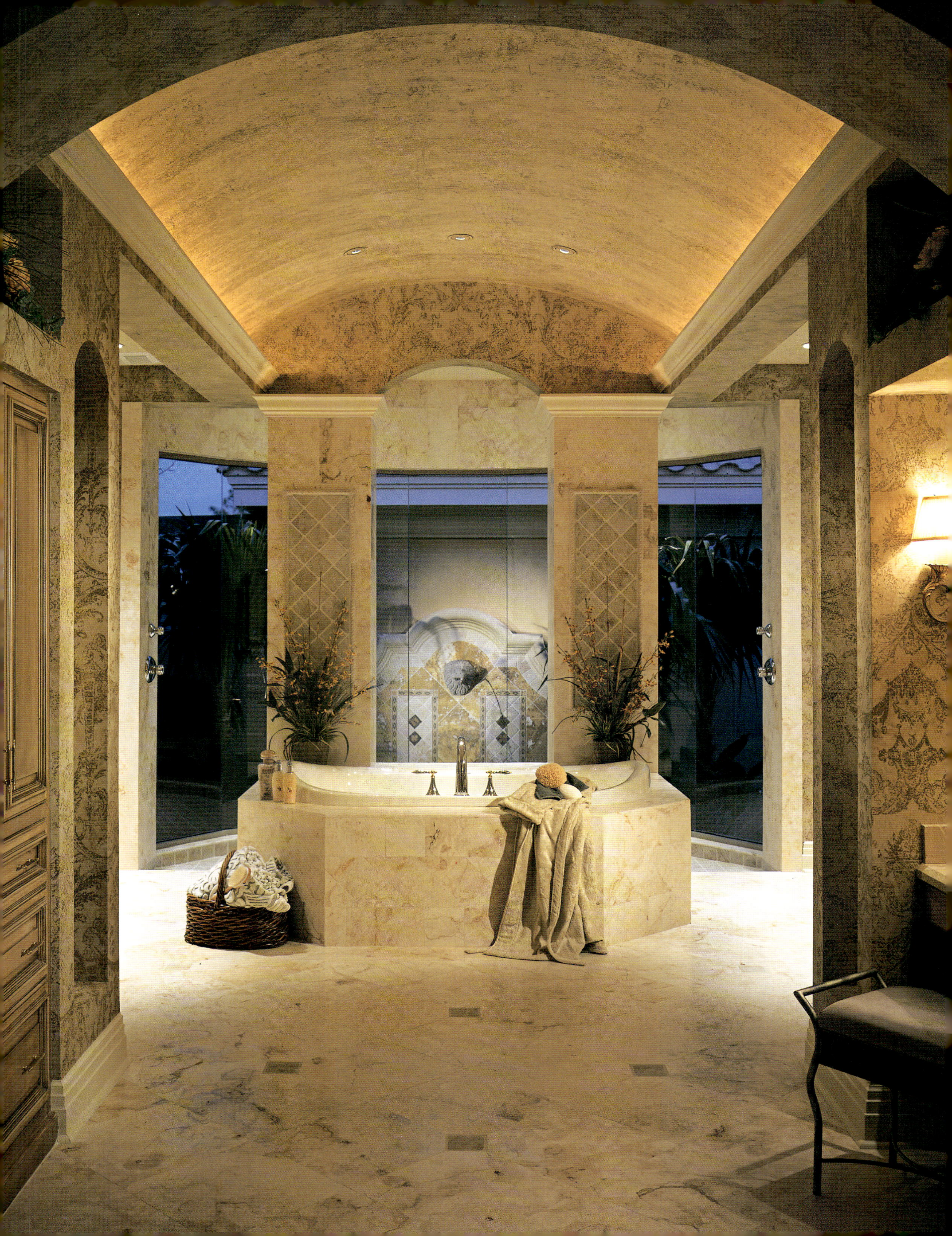

Opposite

COLLINS & DUPONT
INTERIORS, INC.
SHERRON P. DUPONT, ASID

In this master bath, the designer creates drama with a barrel vaulted ceiling, fauxed and papered for textural interest, and by floating the soaking tub. Two supporting columns, trimmed with tumbled stone, separate and frame the shower and accent the views of the private garden and fountain. On the exterior privacy wall, patterns and material complement the interior space as they provide a backdrop for the fountain.

Photo credit: Laurence Taylor

Above

ROBB & STUCKY
SHERRILL HANSON, ASID, IDS,
FLORIDA LICENSED
INTERIOR DESIGNER

Greek and Italian influences imbue an Olde World feel in this beautiful bath. Trompe l'oeil throughout renders the look of stone block, over which flowering vines drape. A gold leaf mirror and gold fixtures adorn the classic pedestal sink.

Photo credit: Barry J. Grossman

MASTER BATH   99

Above

ACCESSORIES ETC., INC.

This master bath is inspired by classical designs with pillars leading the eye upward toward the Palladian window that crowns the room. The curve of the window is repeated with the arched, barrel vault, 16-foot ceiling with hand painted frescos of the blue sky and clouds. His-and-her vanities in rich-hued wood tones and an Oriental rug foster the warmth that contrasts the stonework throughout. (*Builder, Kurtz Homes*)

Photo credit: CJ Walker

Opposite

ACCESSORIES, ETC., INC.

Keystone arches and columns create private niches in this expansive, luxurious and classic bath. The combination of keystone, natural marble, and honey-toned wood cabinetry create an unusual blend of luxurious components. The cabinetry is repeated on either side with his-and-her vanity areas; hers is accented by the addition of an elegant dressing table. A walk-in shower and separate his-and-her toilet rooms complete the suite. (*Builder, Kurtz Homes*)

Photo credit: CJ Walker

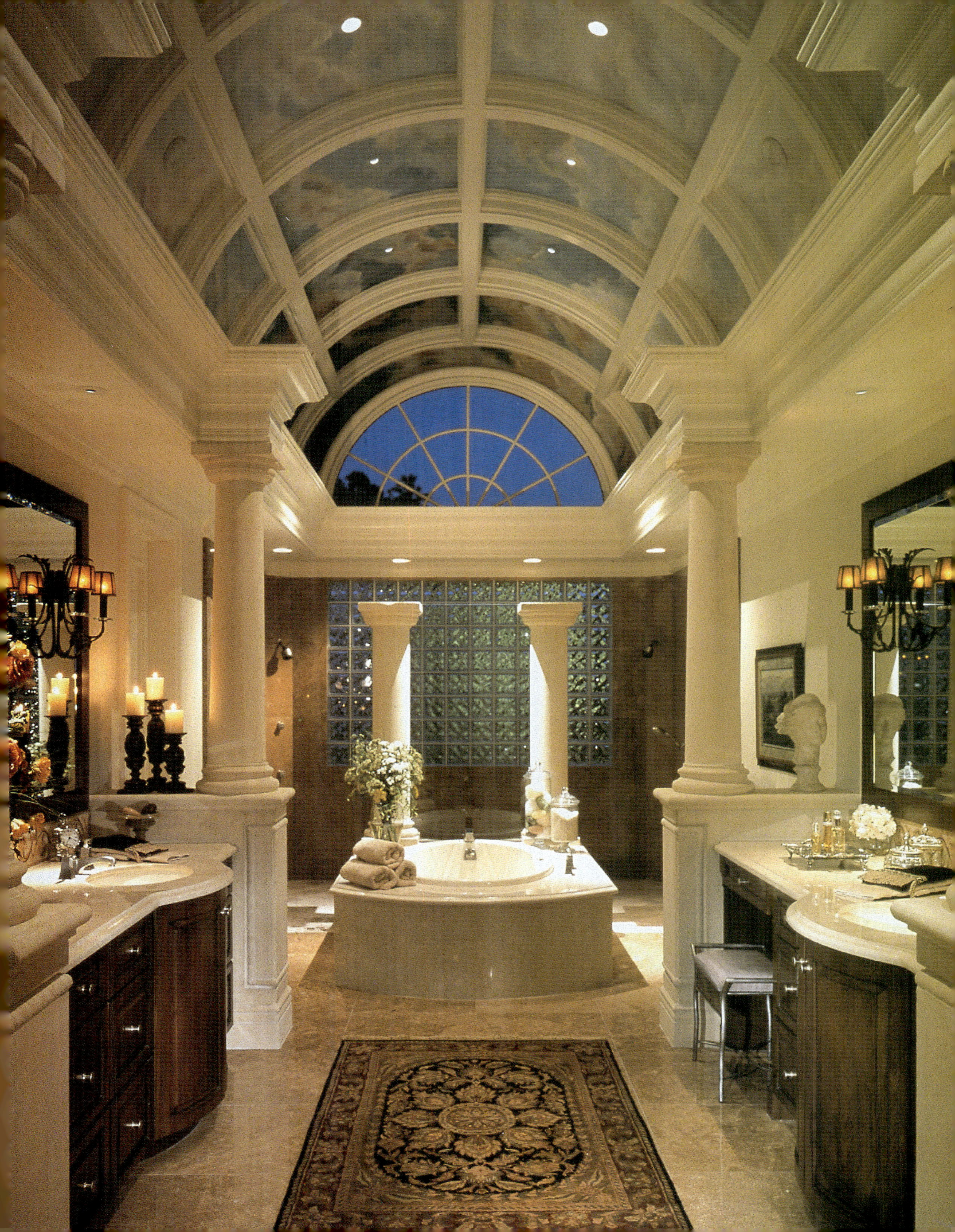

Right

K2 DESIGN GROUP, INC.
JENNY L. CARTER, ASID,
IIDA, ASSOC. AIA

No inside, no outside, the two truly become one in this tropical, modern, Zen-like master bath. A tranquil background and hypnotic waterfall sounds outside add to the gentle spills of the limestone bowls mounted on the wall. Crema Europa limestone curves and angles to form a luxurious retreat, which is reminiscent of beach sand, tidal movement.

Photo credit: Oscar Thompson

Below

LINDY THOMAS INTERIORS
LINDY THOMAS, ASID

The lady of the house has everything she desires in her sophisticated British Colonial style bath with custom, shell stone soaking tub and surround. Aged brass sconces on the mirror and an antique blanket rack for her towels add gentility to the room. Custom cabinets hold everything close by, and the feminine boudoir chair in English chintz makes it unmistakably her bath.

Photo credit: Greg Wilson

Opposite

ROBB & STUCKY
JOSEPHINE ALAIMO, ASID, IDS,
FLORIDA LICENSED
INTERIOR DESIGNER

Neoclassic, understated elegance rejuvenated this redesigned bath. Natural colors of travertine and granite are accented with subtle ivory tones and light olive hues. Neutral and peaceful, this bath with its sensual window treatment and alluring chaise creates a quiet and romantic retreat.

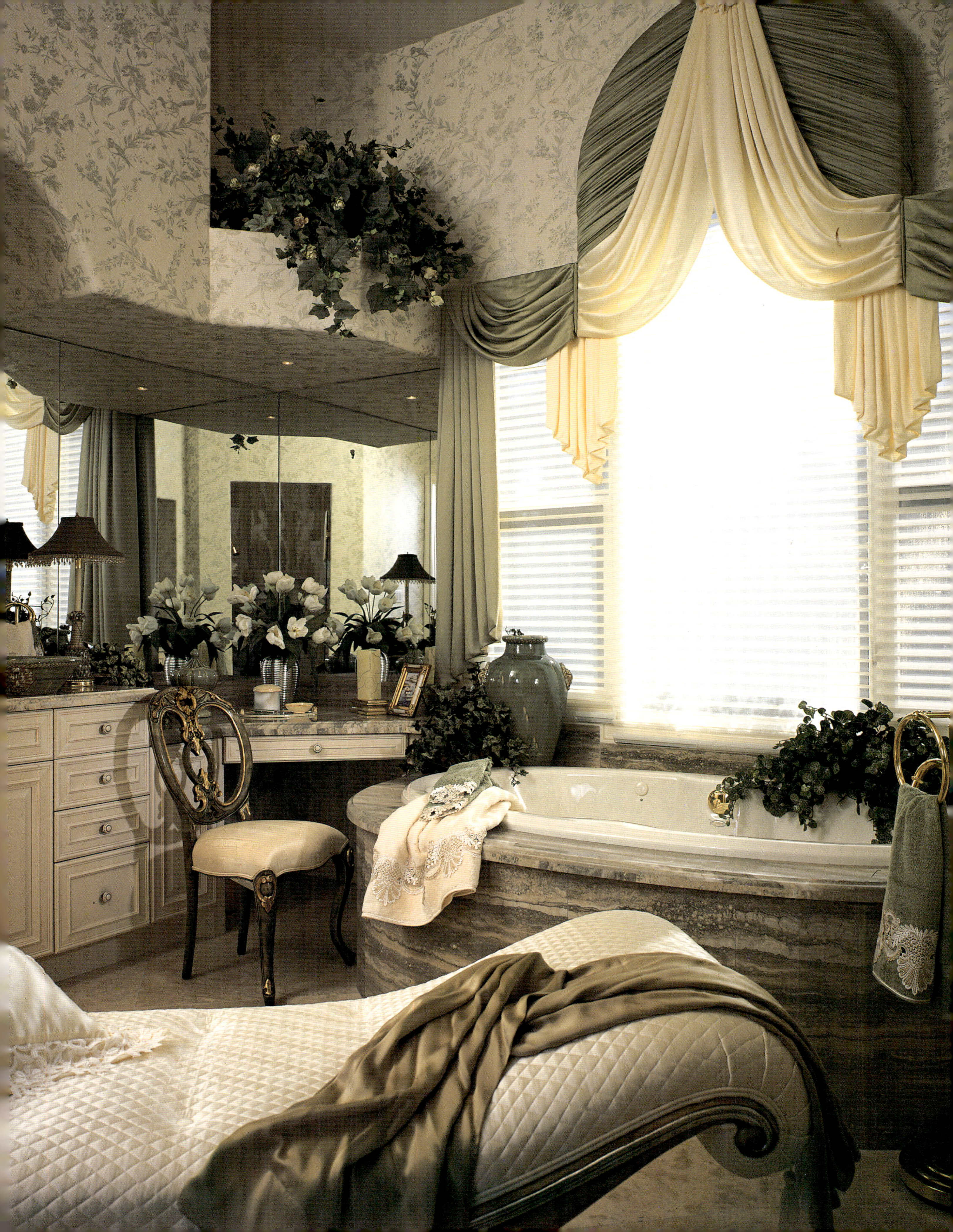

COLLINS & DUPONT
INTERIORS, INC.
SHERRON P. DUPONT, ASID

Rich woods and great stone underfoot create the perfect backdrop for this unique bathroom. A spacious vanity with knee space is topped with a warmly colored granite. Custom designed and finished display cabinets for a collection of miniature shoes and purses anchor each end. Rich fabric, vivid art, and strong color on the walls reiterate that this is Florida.

The view of the master bath at right highlights a deep soaking tub, skirted in the same marble as the main floor, and artfully set into a bay of tall windows. One level up between the tub and windows, a large marble planter forms a privacy wall, lush with tropical vegetation.

Photo credit: Laurence Taylor

MASTER BATH   105

Right

THERESA CAROLLO INTERIORS
THERESA A. CAROLLO,
ALLIED ASID

This master bath is a beautiful exercise in symmetry. The luxurious detail is enhanced with faux finished columns in tones of taupe, cream, and silver, framing a heated Jacuzzi tub. The barrel ceiling is faux finished and crowned with an alabaster chandelier. Double vanities with Saturnia tops showcase the cream cabinetry and stone flooring. This retreat is elegant, functional and inviting.

Photo credit: Ron Blakeley

Below

THERESA CAROLLO INTERIORS
THERESA A. CAROLLO,
ALLIED ASID

Designed for the spa experience, this master bath offers a walk-around, four-head shower that features an all glass view of a private garden. The heated Jacuzzi is accented with a hand-painted trompe l'oeil of an Italian garden. Separate his-and-her vanities allow for individualized pampering. The crown molding set about the mirrored walls houses rope lighting for additional mood experiences.

Photo credit: Ron Blakeley

Opposite

VINCE MULLER
INTERIOR DESIGN
DENISE WARD, ASID

A formalized version of West Indies styling, this master bath utilizes the varying colors in the onyx countertops to provide a palette for the space. Reflected in the stone work, light fixtures, and faucets, the influence is clear. A mixture of honed travertine and tumbled stone in the shower and tub deck lightens the room. (*Builder, Hunt Construction*)

Photo credit: Joseph Lapeyra Photography

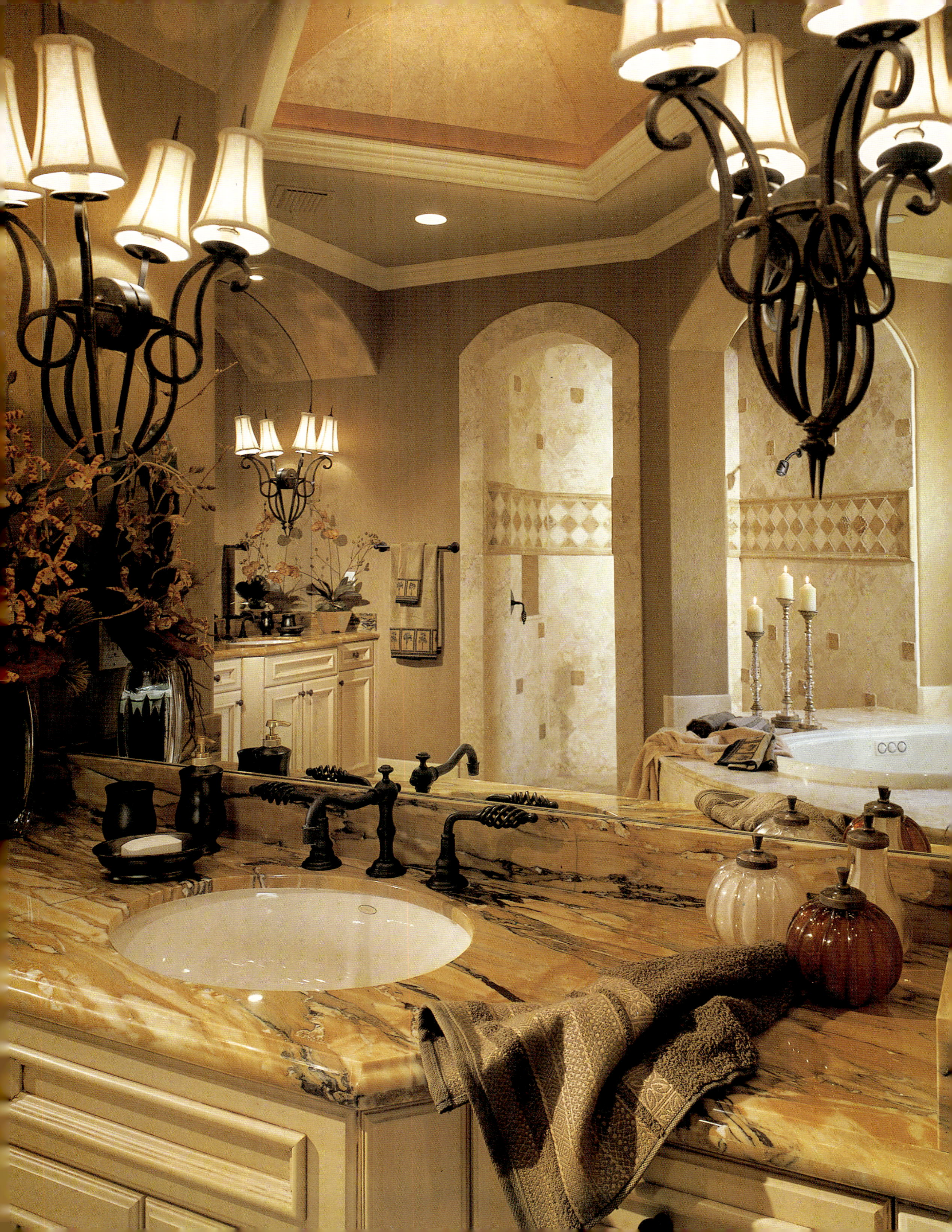

108 ~ FINE INTERIORS OF NAPLES, FLORIDA

Left

**HOLLAND SALLEY
INTERIOR DESIGN
LISA FICARRA SHEPHERD,
ALLIED MEMBER, ASID**

This design concept combines the unique influence of French and Italian details with one of the most distinctive enclaves in the nation. The master bath of this palatial yet comfortable home features a mosaic which conveys a feeling of Olde World timelessness when mixed with the warmth of the dark, custom cabinetry. An expansive walk-in shower, located behind the Roman tub, utilizes inlaid tiles reflecting the colors of the mosaic.

Photo credit: Jennifer Deane

Below

**HUNT CONSTRUCTION CO., INC.
VINCE-MULLER INTERIOR DESIGN**

Created for a spa-like experience, this bath utilizes the beauty of stained and leaded glass to highlight focal points and provide privacy. A walk-in shower, steam room, and seating area adjacent to the spa tub flow seamlessly due to symmetrical arched design and rod iron detailing incorporated above the stone arches.

Photo credit: Joseph Lapeyra Photography

Opposite

**THE THOMAS RILEY
ARTISANS' GUILD
ROMANZA INTERIOR DESIGN**

Intricate hand-carvings adorn the vanity cabinetry and tub moldings of this luxurious woman's bath. All of the cabinetry, panel work, moldings and trib were fabricated and artfully finished in paint and glaze by craftsmen at The Thomas Riley Artisans' Guild. This exceptional woodworking features a bow front vanity and curved window and door casings. Applied moldings decorate the panel work, ceiling design and stately tub surround. Form fits beautifully with function in this elegant and serene refuge.

Photo credit: Laurence Taylor

MASTER BATH

Right

GEARY DESIGN, INC.
RICHARD F. GEARY III

A true minimalist expression, this master bath features clean, spacious vanities on each side of the room. The walk-in shower promotes a seamless experience with the outdoors, offering an abundance of natural light and a view of the surrounding wooded area.

Below

PLATINUM COAST
ARTISANS AND CRAFTSMEN

The beauty and regal quality of mahogany wood has been achieved through professional artistry and unique finishes. Raised panel cabinets in this master bath have been antiqued and glazed to simulate deep mahogany, thus promoting a West Indies feel.

Opposite

THE THOMAS RILEY
ARTISANS' GUILD

A sleek and sophisticated bath is created with black granite vanities and burl wood cabinetry. The black jetted tub serves as an anchor to the room which is surrounded with warm paneled walls, a stippled gold ceiling, and accents of copper, bronze, and onyx.

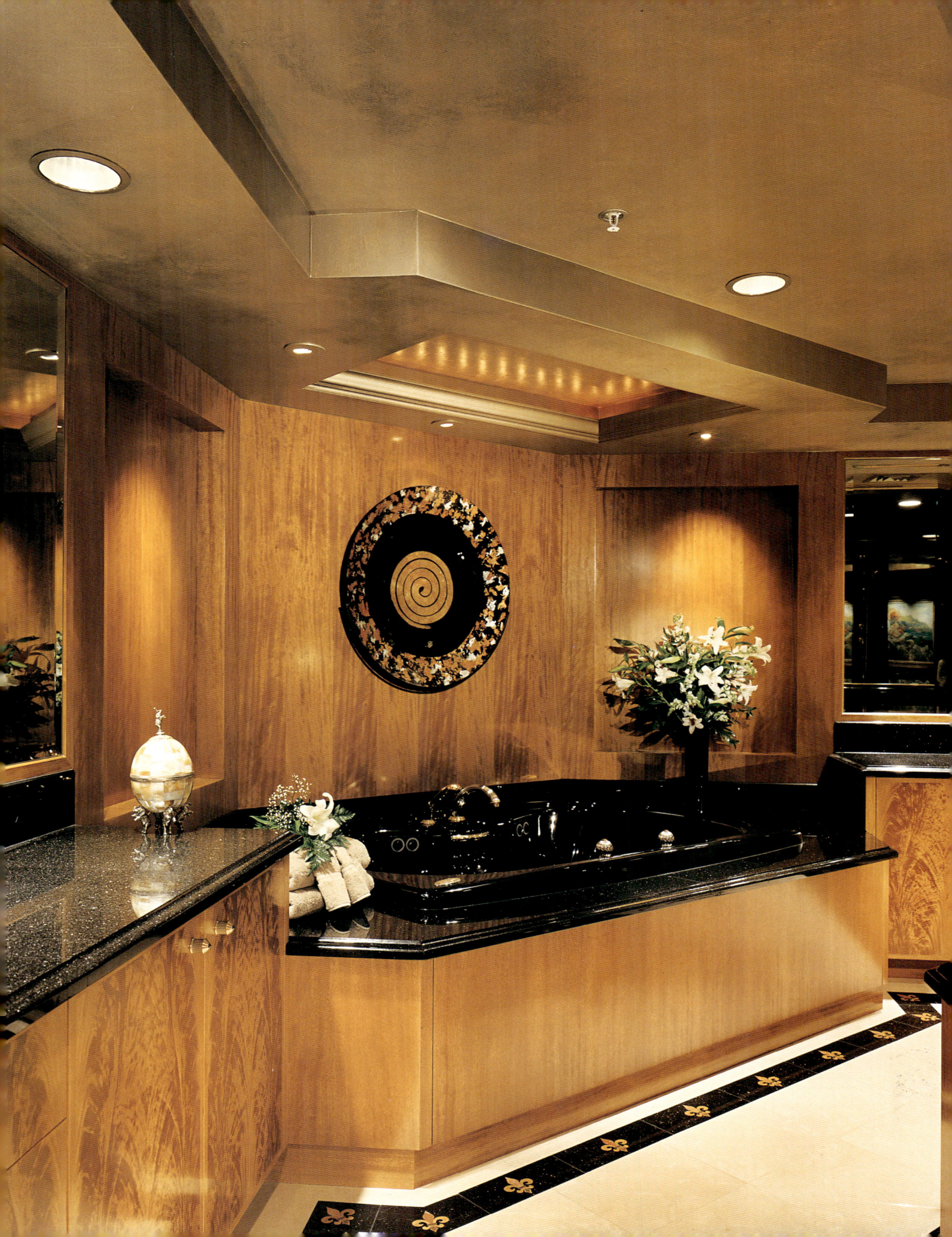

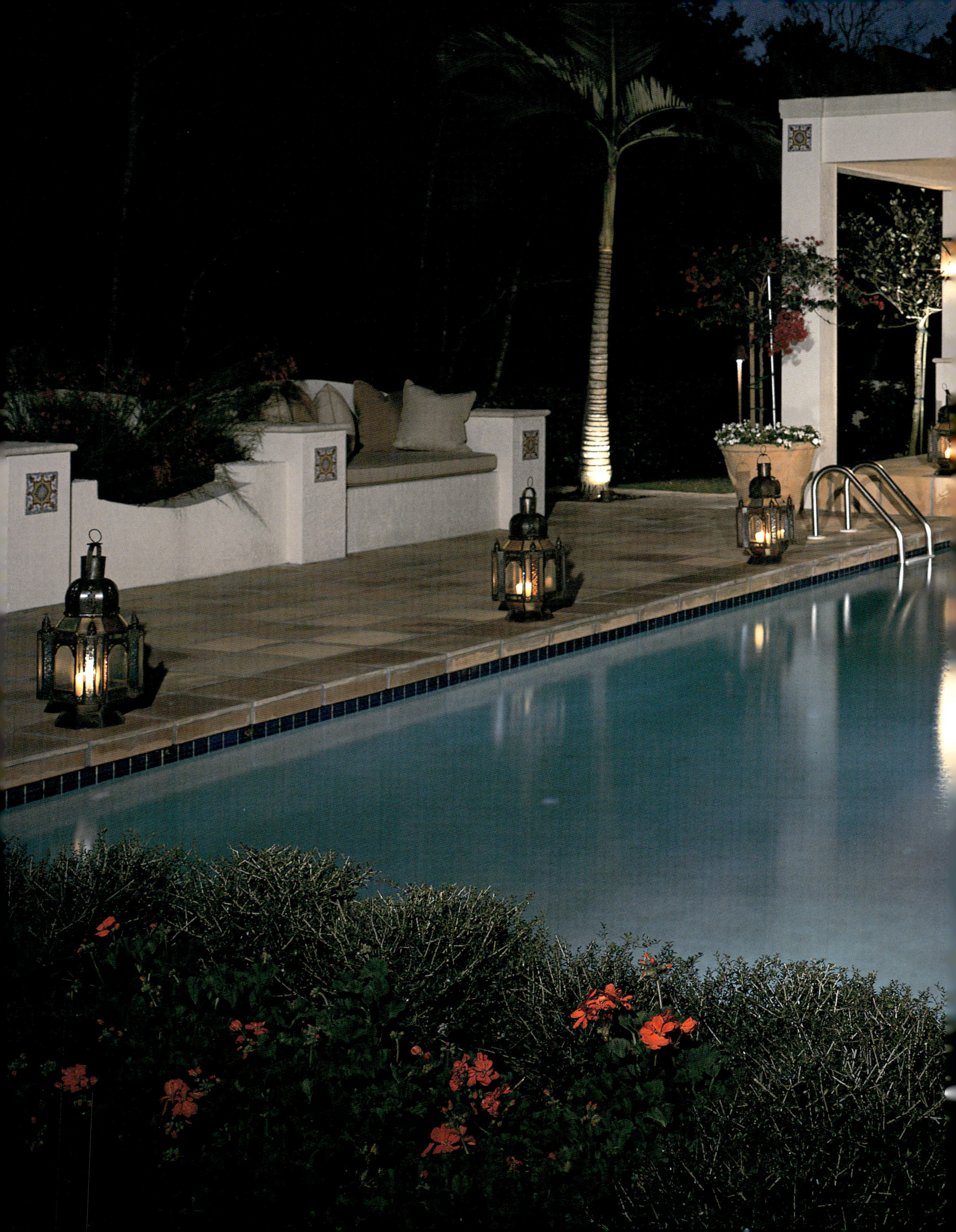

OUTDOOR PATIO

COLLINS & DUPONT
INTERIORS, INC
SHERRON P. DUPONT, ASID

Feeling a bit like a deluxe spa, the spacious pool and patio includes multiple banquette seating and lounging areas. A raised platform of banquettes with a myriad of colorful pillows at the narrow end of the pool is accentuated by a stucco and wood planked pergola. Lantern-like sconces provide soft, sensual lighting while their design details complement the tile insets on the pergola and banquettes.

Photo credit: Laurence Taylor

ACCESSORIES ETC., INC.

Inspired by the classically designed gardens of the Olde World, this outdoor amenity area is the perfect retreat to enjoy the Southwest Florida weather. The Roman pool surrounded by statues and lush vegetation creates a seamless transition between the home's outdoor amenities and its natural setting. (*Builder, Kurtz Homes*)

Photo credit: CJ Walker

DON EWY CONSTRUCTION, INC.

This open and airy cabana with its vast panorama of Gulf views, transports owners and guests to idyllic island-style living. Whether sipping a piña colada at the bar or relaxing near the fireplace, this Mediterranean beachside retreat keeps life simple and carefree.

Photo credit: Dyehouse Comeriato

ROBB & STUCKY
BETTI WALCOTT, ASID, IDS,
INTERIOR DESIGNER

Family activity and outdoor living has never been so appealing. In this custom-designed pool, the elevated spa, adorned with planters, spills continuously over the waterfall's edge. The stone tile deck provides a natural environment. Stylish and comfortable Braxton Culler seating ensures the ultimate in relaxation.

OUTDOOR PATIO   117

Left

THERESA CAROLLO INTERIORS
THERESA A. CAROLLO,
ALLIED ASID

As seen from the far side near the bar and grill, this lanai and pool area is designed to accommodate outdoor livability. A classic gazebo "floats" on the edge of the pool near the rock garden and waterfall spa. Overstuffed wicker and iron upholstered seating, and stone mosaic tables complement the entertaining areas.

Photo credit: Ron Blakeley

Opposite

A semicircular stone waterfall spills into the spa and then cascades into a stylish deck adorned with natural slate, pedestal-style stools. Ideal for sun and cool relaxation, the three-tiered pool/spa combination offers a variety of splashy options.

Photo credit: Ron Blakeley

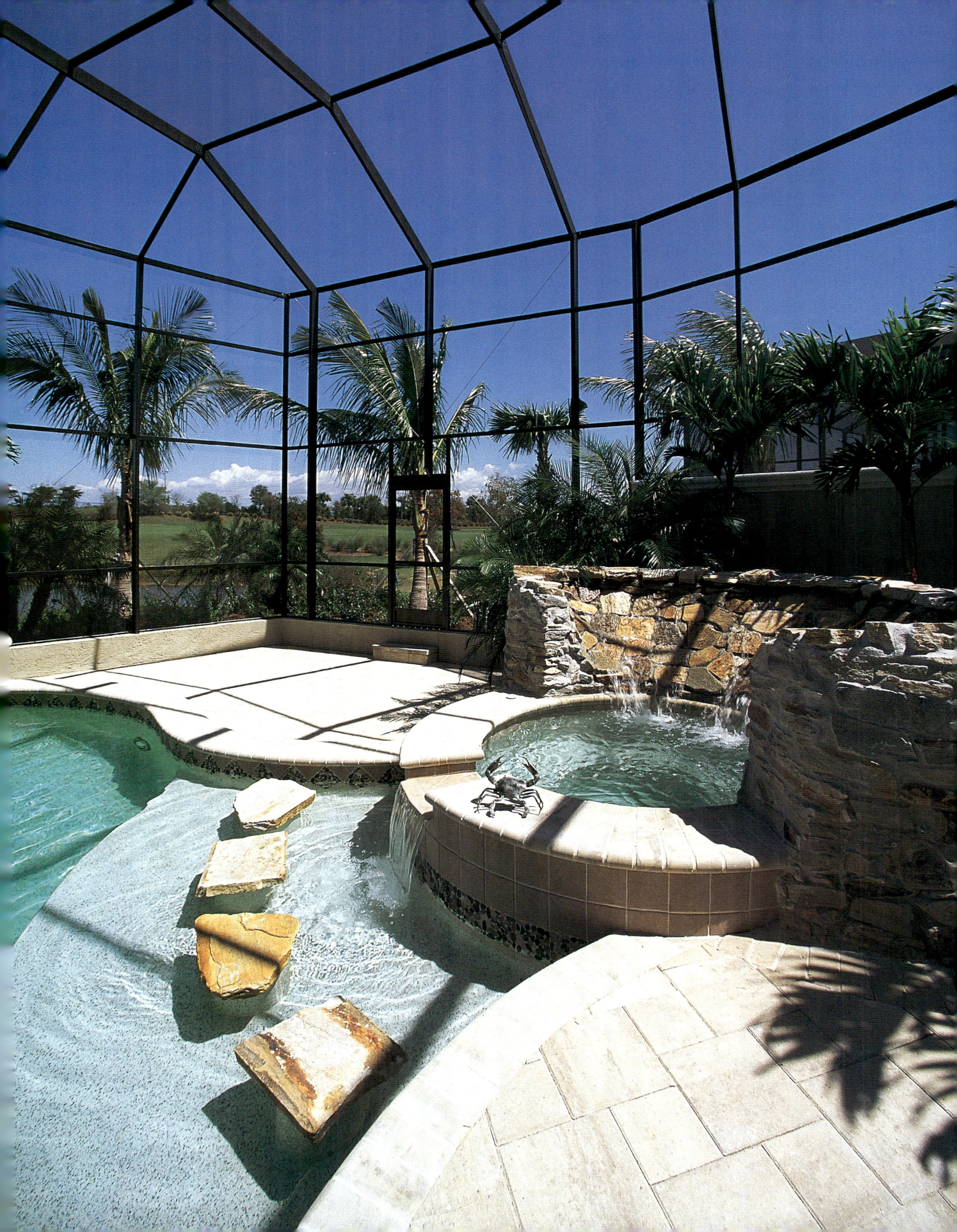

Above

GEARY DESIGN INC.
RICHARD F. GEARY III

The pool area is tucked inside this u-shaped construction and gives the bathers total privacy, yet allows for plenty of sun. The fixed glass window at the end of the pool offers a view of the owner's exotic car collection. The teak chaise lounges can be wheeled out into the sun or tucked under the covered area.

Photo credit: Ed Chappell

Opposite

COLLINS & DUPONT
INTERIORS, INC.
KIM COLLINS, ASID

This retreat imbues al fresco dining with a Provencal flair. An octagonal wood ceiling with indirect lighting accentuates the shape of this wonderful patio area. The wood mantle connects the built-in cabinetry above to the marble-faced fireplace, and the bronzed metal table and chairs lend a patina of age to the entire scene.

Photo credit: Laurence Taylor

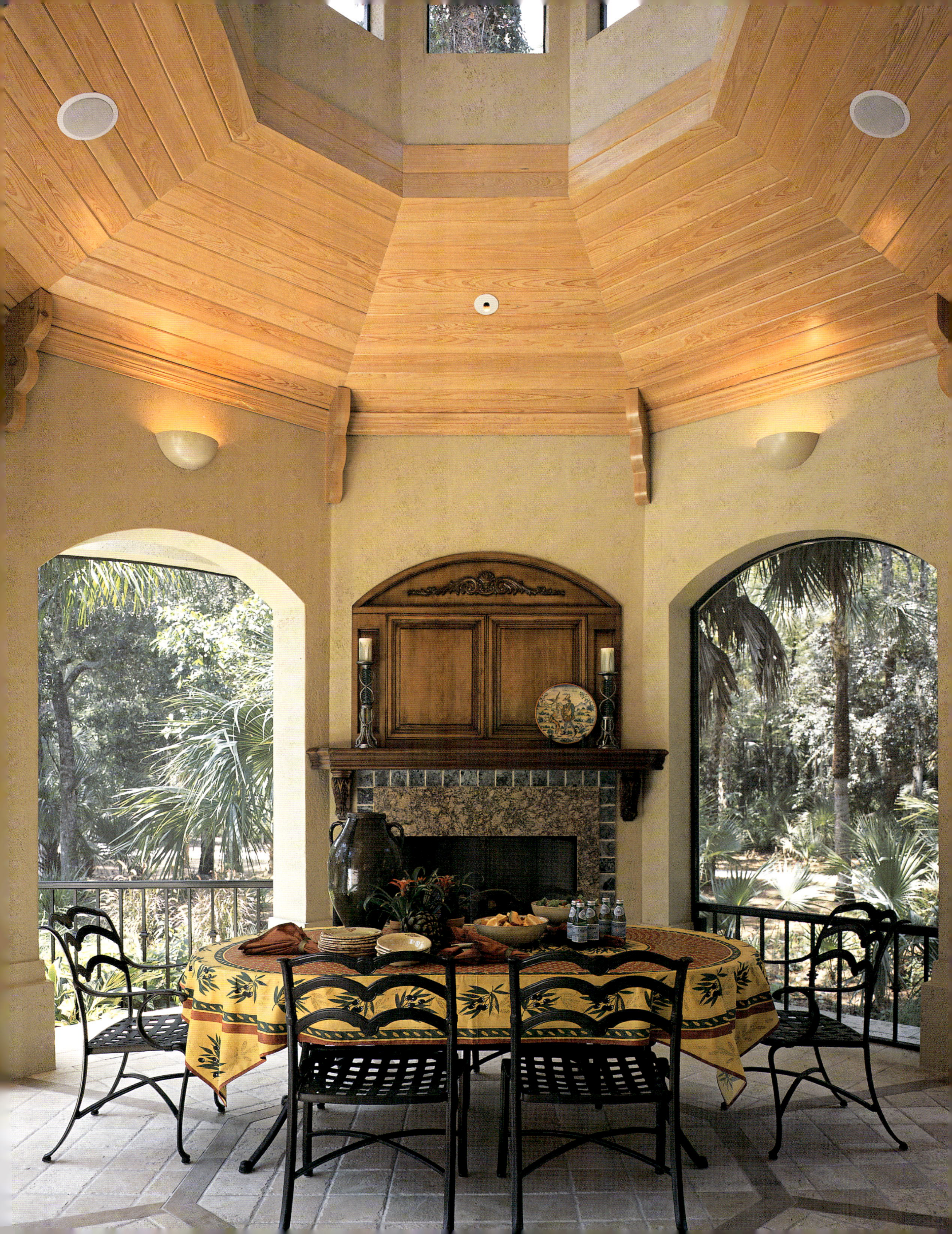

Above

GEARY DESIGN INC.
RICHARD F. GEARY III

This fully screened entertainment patio boasts an outdoor fireplace, seating area, and dining space. The table passes through the glass divider to bring the inside out and the outside in. Cool in the summer and cozy in the winter, it allows for outdoor enjoyment any time of the year. This area is also part of the loggia that connects the main house with the guest suite and offers access to the pool.

Photo credit: Dan Forer

Opposite

ROBB & STUCKY
SHERRILL HANSON, ALLIED MEMBER, ASID, IDS,
FLORIDA LICENSED
INTERIOR DESIGNER

Redesigned from highly contemporary to traditional with an Indies' flair, this home's outdoor area is designed to be an extension of the interior design's features. Exotic wood in the ceiling complements metal, stone, and neutral textiles. Bronze cast aluminum frames and seating woven to resemble indoor linen upholstery renders Olde World charm. An oval table with mosaic top and delicate botanicals provides additional interest.

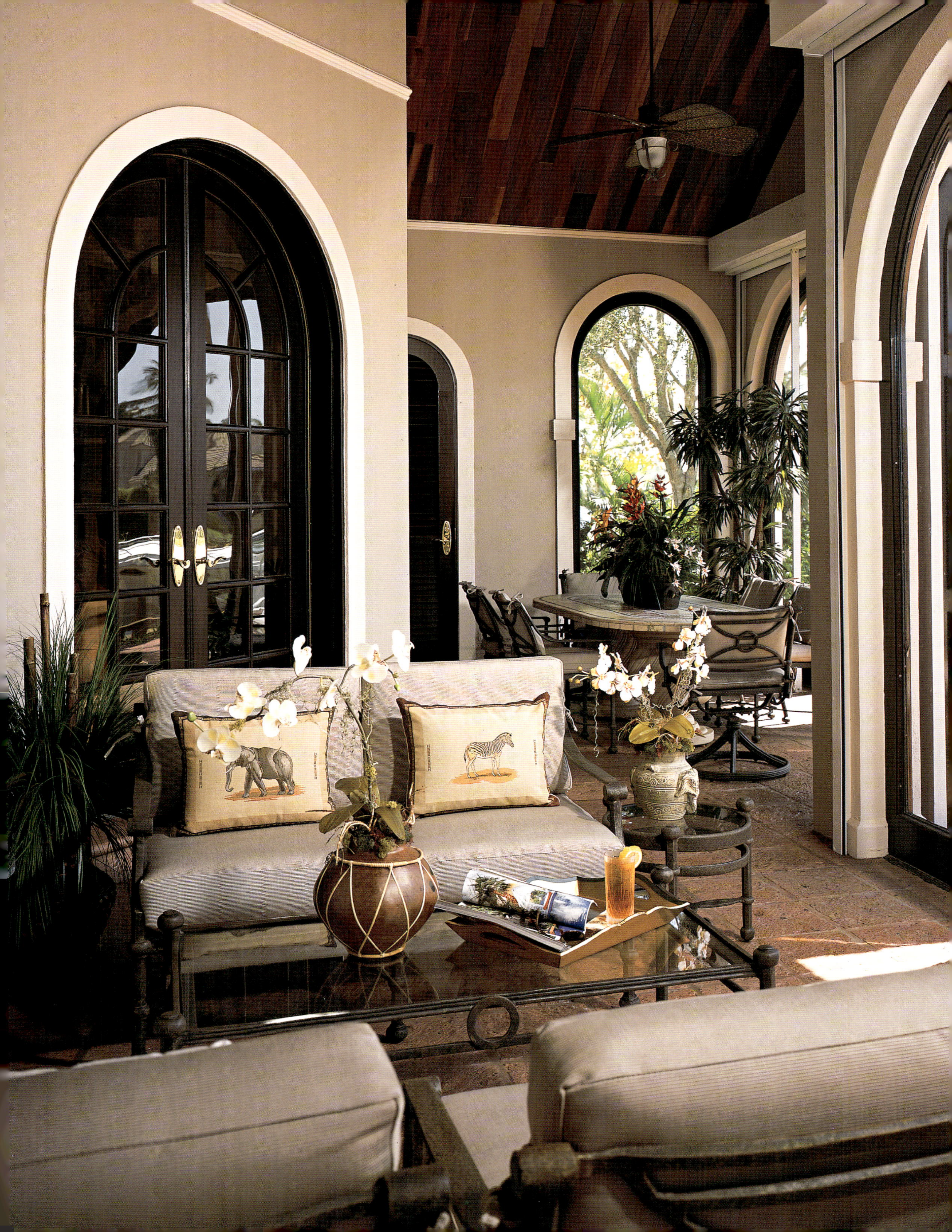

HUNT CONSTRUCTION CO., INC.
Brunch is served in this expansive outdoor living area that soars two-stories and provides a variety of living spaces. Chenille-cushioned, rattan and wicker chairs surround the dining table created from a combination of faux stone bases and a natural stone top. A three-tiered waterfall spills from the elevated spa.

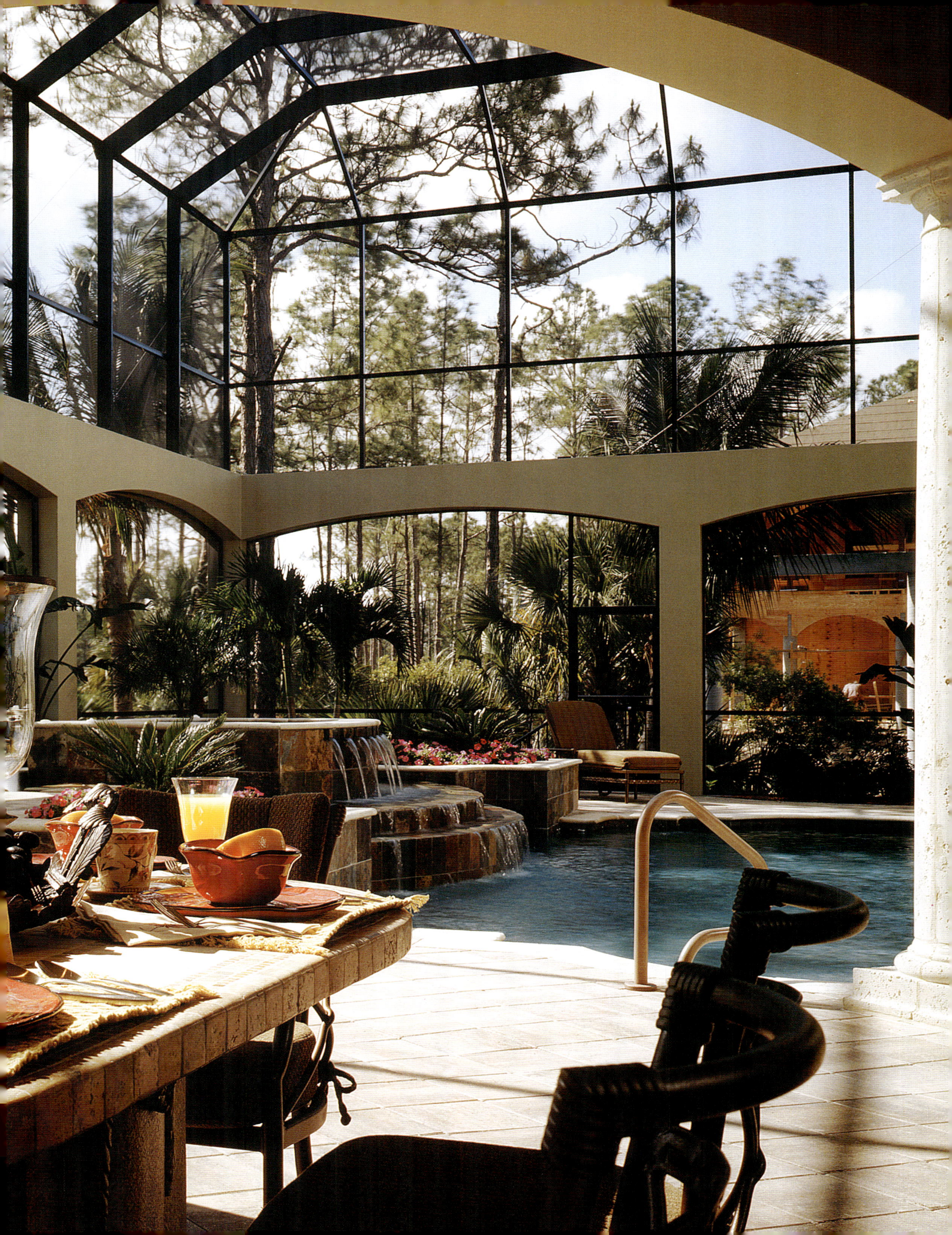

ROMANZA INTERIOR DESIGN
MARNIE SORENSEN

Textured stone and natural fibers combine to make this outdoor living space both cozy and cool. A uniquely positioned, two-sided fireplace serves as a focal point for both the summer kitchen and the adjacent lanai. Both spaces are covered by a warm, cedar tongue-and-groove ceiling. (*Builder, London Bay Homes*)

Photo credit: Laurence Taylor.

126   FINE INTERIORS OF NAPLES, FLORIDA

ROMANZA INTERIOR DESIGN
NATALIE SORRENTINO

One of the most desirable and appealing design elements to have emerged in multi-million dollar homes is the loggia: a spacious under-roof, outdoor living area. Bounding with amenities of a summer kitchen and fireplace, this living and dining area presents the finest elements of Florida living.

Photo credit: Laurence Taylor

CONTRIBUTORS

Accessories, Etc., Inc.
9696 Bonita Beach Road, Suite 101
Bonita Springs, Florida 34135
accessoriesetc@hotmail.com
front cover, 1, 10, 13, 31, 45, 52, 53, 64, 66, 74, 78, 89, 100, 101, 115

Collins & DuPont Interiors, Inc.
8911 Brighton Lane
Bonita Springs, Florida 34135
11, 17, 26, 88, 98, 104, 105, 112–113, 114, 121

Design Group West
9115 Galleria Court
Naples, Florida 34109
23, 37, 40, 50, 54

Don Ewy Construction, Inc.
8005 Vera Cruz Way
Naples, Florida 34109
13, 15, 62, 116

Freestyle Interiors
8800 Signal Road, Suite 1
Bonita Springs, Florida 34135
www.freestyleinteriors.com
12, 26, 40, 64

Geary Design, Inc.
5353 Jaeger Road
Naples, Florida 34109
www.gearydesign.com
58, 60, 94, 110, 120, 122

Holland Salley, Inc.
Residential & Commercial
Interior Design
Design Studio & Showroom
2975 South Horseshoe Drive,
Suite 800
Naples, Florida 34104
design@hollandsalley.com
10, 16, 17, 28, 30, 41, 43, 50, 53, 85, 94, 109

Hunt Construction Co., Inc.
4061 Bonita Beach Road, #201
Bonita Springs, FL 34134
back cover, 3, 5, 6–7, 9, 20–21, 23, 65, 70–71, 73, 93, 109, 124–125

Jinx McDonald Designs, Inc.
Edgemont Office Park
5603 Naples Boulevard
Naples, Florida 34109
76, 90

K2 Design Group, Inc.
3940 Radio Road, Sutie 102
Naples, Florida 34104
44, 56–57, 59, 67, 74, 86, 95, 102

Lindy Thomas Interiors
5405 Taylor Road, Suite 5
Naples, Florida 34109
Lingymt@earthlink.net
19, 27, 28, 35, 45, 80(2), 102

London Bay Homes
9130 Galleria Court , Suite 200
Naples, Florida 34109
info@londonbay.com
60

Lundin Interiors, Inc.
1042 Pine Ridge Road
Naples, Florida 34108
24, 32–33, 35, 55, 84

Nancy Hannigan Fine Art Studio
2453 Sunset Avenue
Naples, Florida 34112
68

Platinum Coast Artisans
and Craftsmen
3435 Enterprise Avenue
Naples, Florida 34104
www.platinumcoastartisans.com
24, 63, 67, 110

Robb & Stucky
Corporate Offices
13170 South Cleveland Avenue
Fort Myers, Florida 33907
back cover, 8, 9, 25, 34, 37, 49, 54, 59, 77, 87, 96–97, 99, 103, 117, 123

Romanza Interior Design
2016 Trade Center Way,
Suite F
Naples, Florida 34109
38(2), 42, 61, 68, 75, 79, 126, 127

Roz Travis Interiors, Inc.
1810 J and C Boulevard
Naples, Florida 34103
18, 48, 93

The Thomas Riley
Artisans' Guild
1510 Railhead Boulevard
Naples, Florida 34110
www.artisansguild.net
14(2), 30, 72, 73, 81, 108, 111

Theresa Carollo, Allied ASID
853 Vanderbilt Beach Road
Naples, Florida 34108
36, 39, 63, 69, 76, 86, 90, 106(2), 118, 119

Valentine & Stone Interiors
4450 Bonita Beach Road
Bonita Springs, Florida 34134
back cover, 22, 43, 51, 82–83, 85, 91

Vince Muller Interior Design
8870 Emerald Isle, Suite 103
Bonita Springs, Florida 34135
29, 46–47, 49, 89, 92, 107